WAY

OF THE

REAPER

ALSO BY
NICHOLAS IRVING

The Reaper

WAY
OF THE
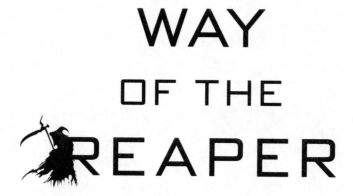# REAPER

MY GREATEST UNTOLD MISSIONS
AND THE ART OF BEING A SNIPER

NICHOLAS IRVING
WITH GARY BROZEK

ST. MARTIN'S PRESS 🔠 NEW YORK

www.stmartins.com

Designed by Steven Seighman

The Library of Congress Cataloging-in-Publication Data is available upon request.

ISBN 978-1-250-08835-2 (hardcover)
ISBN 978-1-250-08836-9 (e-book)

Our books may be purchased in bulk for promotional, educational, or business use. Please contact your local bookseller or Macmillan Corporate and Premium Sales Department at 1-800-221-7945, extension 5442, or by e-mail at MacmillanSpecial Markets@macmillan.com.

First Edition: August 2016

10 9 8 7 6 5 4 3 2 1

To the fallen men of the 75th Ranger Regiment and, in particular, Ben Kopp and Anibal Santiago

TABLE OF CONTENTS

Author's Note   ix

1. Band of Brothers Plays at the Hotel Party   1
2. Think First, Ask Questions, and Then Fire   35
3. The Virtues of Patience   57
4. Someone to Watch over Us   77
5. Finding Your Focus on a Hell Night in Helmand   99
6. Without Remorse   143
7. Keeping Track of Yourself   167
8. Timing Is Everything   197
9. Missing the Action   223
10. After Action Report   249

PREFACE

When I sat down to write my first book, *The Reaper,* I had a couple of goals in mind. One of them was obvious: to share my experiences as a sniper and to reveal how it was that I was able to score so many kills—thirty-three—in such a short period of time. If you've read that book then you know that a lot of my success was due to my being in the right place at the right time. Our operational tempo was very high during that period in Afghanistan in 2009. A lot of other highly skilled snipers in the Rangers simply didn't get the opportunity that I had. I'm a huge sports fan, and football is my main game, and in some ways I'd like to think that I was the young, untested quarterback who came in to replace the injured starter. I got lucky and had some early success and the coach decided to go with the hot hand and ride that streak of good fortune and good execution for as long as he could. The truth is, that wasn't exactly the case. Yes, I did get off to a good start and all of that, but it was just our unit's good luck that when the time came for us to roll on out, we encountered the enemy.

I'm pretty sure that if any of the other snipers besides me had gone out there, they would have gotten the job done. That's not being modest, that's just the truth of it. The kind of close-action sniping that made up the majority of those kills is very different from the long-distance/long-range sniping that a lot of people associate with the specialized work that snipers do. Sure, I had to do some calculations and rely on my spotter for information, but, except in rare cases, I wasn't out there alone for days on end essentially by myself. I'm not a lone-wolf kind of guy. I like being with my pack and I know that for as much as I had their backs and was working my ass off to protect them, my teammates were there for me.

For that reason, I wanted to share more of my experiences with you. If you've read *The Reaper*, then you've already gotten the basics of my career in the military: my background as the son of a military man and a military woman, and how I was fortunate to become a proud member of the finest fighting force out there—the

Rangers—after first serving in various capacities as a Stryker driver and machine gunner, then enrolling in Sniper School, and eventually rising to the role of Sniper Team Leader.

The focus of those earlier stories was always going to be on that extraordinary period in 2009 when I worked in the Special Operations community as a Ranger. I use the word "extraordinary" in the purest sense—it was beyond the normal in terms of intensity compared with what a lot of deployments, including many of my others, were like. The truth is that missions aren't successful, battles aren't won, just by the guys at the point of the spear. The "Rangers Lead the Way," as the motto goes, but a lot of other people put them out front and back them up. It takes an incredible amount of teamwork and support from every level to get the job done. A lot of times, that work isn't very glamorous and won't grab any headlines or become a sound bite on the news. It will rarely be the subject of a question from an audience member at a book signing or to a radio call-in program.

Don't get me wrong. I'm not saying that the work isn't dangerous, that the adrenaline isn't pumping, or anything like that.

I know that a lot of times when someone achieves something that's worth noting, it's almost as if he's an overnight success. I don't think that anybody ever succeeds without having to pay the price along the way, without having to learn more than a few lessons, sometimes from great teachers and sometimes the hard way—through experience.

The stories that I want to share with you span my entire military career and reflect a wide variety of the experiences I had and some of the lessons I learned during the six years I proudly served. That said, they don't include every one of my proudest moments. I should clarify that a bit. I'm proud of the work that I did in my six-year career in the Army. I didn't always perform at my absolute best, but that's on me and not the people I worked with—the team leaders, platoon commanders, and others who put me in the position where I could succeed or fail. When I had that run of good fortune in 2009, I was twenty-three years old, but I'd been in the military for five years. That means that I'd had a lot of time and opportunity to learn a few things.

I'm proud to say that before I became a member of the sniper team I served as a member of the weapons squad for a long time. My days as a machine gunner really helped me to see the big picture, to be able to understand the tactical side of operations, to get a feel for how our enemies would operate in both an urban and a rural environment. I wasn't always staring down the scope of Dirty Diana, my SR-25 weapon. I'd done a lot of other things before I earned my spot as a sniper. I was eighteen years old when I entered the Army; working with weapons was like being turned loose in a toy store. I appreciated what a .50-caliber machine gun could do—how deadly it could be—but still it was a whole lot of fun having that kind of power in my hands.

It was funny that for each weapon system or other equipment I was being trained on, those lessons were called "school." To me, it was more like recess. Who wouldn't have felt that way when they had their hands on a Mark 47 computer-aided grenade launcher? With that thing I felt like I could put a grenade through an open window damn near a mile away. It was like a sniper rifle that shoots grenades. How cool was that?

Some of the other highlights of my early training were becoming Gustav-qualified. That .84mm Carl Gustav recoilless antitank weapon was amazing. The surreal part of it all was that it wasn't a weapons choice I had from the armory in a video game, I was actually holding it my hands.

Probably the best example of the kind of teamwork that made my days in the weapons squad so memorable was being at the controls of a 20-ton Stryker. I was in charge of maneuvering that giant eight-wheeled armored vehicle, but I had to rely on someone else to give me directions through the streets of Mosul, Iraq. I was nineteen and twenty years old and that kind of power at your disposal is both humbling and thrilling. Thanks to my troop commander, Juan, I was able to keep him and me, and the other nine members of the unit traveling in the Stryker, safe. The Army and my fellow GIs put a lot of trust in me, and as a result I grew up fast, became a more confident and competent individual than I would have been if I'd have gone on to college or gotten a job right out of high school. Having millions of dollars of US government property and the priceless lives of guys you cared about as if they were your brothers will do that for you. The bonds that I formed with many of the guys I served with remain as strong as ever.

Since I've retired from active duty, I miss the camaraderie and I know that there's nothing I will do in my life that will come close to reproducing the feelings I had while at war. This book is a way for me to share those feelings with others again. It's been a real pleasure for me to reflect on those times, places, and lessons that helped make me who I am today. I hope that you enjoy them.

What follows are stories from the battlefields of Iraq and Afghanistan. Rather than present them in chronological order, from my earliest days to my last ones serving this country, I've chosen to present them as a kind of series of memories and impressions. I want to immerse you in the action, but also will occasionally step out of the heat of the moment to give you some additional insights. I believe that this more accurately represents how I continue to experience those memories myself. The war I experienced was seldom sequential and logical and orderly. Even in my recollection of the events, I'm still surprised at how events developed; I'm still puzzling about how to put the entirety of my experiences into a coherent whole.

I trust that I won't try your patience too much as I sort through the pile. I also want to take the opportunity to thank readers who've made my first book a success and have made this second one possible. I'm grateful for the opportunity to have served and to have learned, both while on active duty and as I continue my journey.

The truth of the matter is that you always know the right thing to do. The hard part is doing it.

—GENERAL NORMAN SCHWARZKOPF

ACKNOWLEDGMENTS

No man can become a Ranger without a lot of help. For me, that began at the beginning. Thanks to my mom and dad for helping keep me on the path and teaching me to never give up. They handed me off to many fine men in the Army, particularly my team leaders, who helped mold me into the Ranger I eventually became. Thanks also to my wife, Jessica, who, along with my parents, provided me with amazing support and put up with long periods of separation during my deployments.

I'd also like to thank all the people involved in the making of this book, from my wonderful editor, Marc

Resnick, and his assistant, Jaime Coyne, who helped lead the way, and to all the other people behind the scenes at St. Martin's Press. I'm grateful for the opportunity to share my experiences with readers.

WAY

OF THE

REAPER

ONE

BAND OF BROTHERS PLAYS AT THE HOTEL PARTY

I'M A HANDS-ON LEARNER. I mean no disrespect when I say this, but because of that, I often felt like much of the time I spent back in the States doing classwork assignments was a waste. I know that there were some other guys that I went through various training program with who benefited from watching PowerPoint presentations, but I really didn't. I mean, I sat through them and I understood the information and the strategies that were being discussed, but a lot of times that didn't translate when it came time to perform during an operation while I was downrange in Iraq. It's also important to understand that in those early years of the conflict, we were all learning a lot about urban warfare. Back stateside, we could sit there and have things drawn up for us on paper, but what I learned in that first deployment was that things are sometimes a lot more fluid out on the battlefield. Forgive my play on the word "fluid," considering that some of what I was experiencing on that operation—the fatigue and some of the disorientation and foggy thinking—was due to dehydration.

The higher-ups seemed to understand how important it was for us to have on-job training and how hard it was to simulate that in an exercise. At least in my experience, they tried to ease us into the really nasty shit. Think of it as kind of like how some people prefer to get into a body of water a bit at a time versus those who like to just dive right in. Diving into the middle of hot combat isn't the best thing for anybody—too many lives could be placed at risk. For that reason, a lot of what I and the other new guys did on operations was to sit in one of the vehicles we used to get to a zone and listen on the comms—our communications systems—while the more veteran guys went out and performed. Another way to think of it is like being a rookie on a team or the underclassman who was brought up to play varsity. The coaches expect you to sit there and pay attention and learn from watching, but even that isn't enough to prepare you for how chaotic a firefight can be.

I'm not trying to pin the blame on anybody else for some of my early mistakes. That's not the point. Everybody was doing their best to prepare us, and I was trying to pick the brains of some of the guys coming back who already had three or four deployments under their belts. Even doing that, I wasn't as prepared as I would have liked. I wasn't alone in that. The 75th Regiment, 3rd Ranger Battalion, was undergoing a big change as we moved toward a fast-strike and small-unit strategy. We were adapting methods that other elite units—the SEALS, Delta Force, and other Special Operations (Spec Ops) teams—were utilizing and evolving best practices as time went on. Before I was first deployed, what the Rangers were mostly doing was pulling outer security for Delta Force when they went in and did room-clearing operations. Once we proved that we were capable of doing that, when the Delta Force guys were engaged in other operations we earned the right to take on more of those responsibilities. It was a cool time to be in the Rangers, to see how things were changing, but I can't say that I sensed all of that at the time. I was just glad to be a part of the in-and-out operations that involved enemy captures and kills.

I'd wanted to be involved in combat for so long that I was always pretty impatient and had a hard time following rules. Some of what we were told seemed flat-out stupid—for example, that as machine gunners we shouldn't fire our weapons unless ABSOLUTELY necessary so as not to reveal our weapons strength. Some rules made more sense to me, but I went ahead and violated them anyway. For instance, on one operation I took the suppressor that one of the assaulters never used. He kept it with the rest of his gear, and when we were called out on an operation, I took it and put it on the end of my M4 for no other reason than that I wanted to see what it would be like. Snipers used them all the time, and I wanted to do what they did.

Juan was my team leader at that point and, when he heard the distinctive sound of a suppressed weapon being fired—something that no weapons squad guy had any need to be doing—he gave me the evil eye. He was cool about it, knowing how eager I was and all. Everything would have gone down better if I had immediately put the suppressor back where I'd taken it from. The assaulter—I've long since forgotten his name—came back and was in a panic. He knew he'd catch hell for losing that piece of equipment. Before I could explain anything, his commander was all over him, giving him a dressing-down for losing an item that cost thousands and thousands of dollars.

I did what I had to do. I stepped up and said, "He didn't lose it." I felt like I was going to lose my lunch when the commander glared at me like I'd shit on his shoe or something.

I held out the suppressor. "I took it. I used it."

I knew it was going to take some time for the commander to trust me. I took my punishment like a man, but in the end, things weren't too bad. I better understood what my role was and where the lines were that I wasn't to cross. That didn't mean I didn't ever cross them again, but at least I wasn't so obvious about it. Every soldier needs discipline, but I think that if you turned us all into computers or into some other kind of instruction-and-rule-following machines, we wouldn't be as successful of a military unit as we are. You still need guys to be flexible and to think on their feet and to want to test limits.

I can't say that I looked at it like that when I was a nineteen-year-old kid out there on the pavement in Iraq at our forward operating base in 120-degree temperatures, changing the oil in one of the Strykers. I knew that I sure as hell didn't want to be doing maintenance work like that for the rest of my deployments, so I'd better become a better soldier. That meant paying my dues and not fantasizing so much about where I wanted to end up, but focusing on doing a better job at what I was assigned to presently. That's not easy when you're nineteen—or twenty-nine or thirty-nine, I imagine—but I was going to give it my best shot.

I also knew this, and it didn't take me spending any time in a classroom to understand it. We had to have each other's backs out there. Even when I screwed up and took that suppressor, I knew that I had to step up and admit that I was the one who took it. I couldn't see another guy taking the fall for something I did. From early on in my days in the military and through the end of my time, the bonds that I formed with the guys went deeper than any other relationships I had. That camaraderie and brotherhood was one of the most special parts about serving in the Army, and in Spec Ops that was even truer, because you were dealing with a smaller set of guys. It was one thing to be in boot camp and be all excited about being part of a team, but when you saw that in action out on the battlefield, it was way more impressive. It wasn't so much that you talked about it; you just went out there and lived it. That's the way I liked it.

My second deployment found me in the city of Mosul in 2007. I didn't know a whole lot about Mosul prior to learning that it was our next base of operation. Once I found out where we were headed, I learned a few things to help me prepare for another go downrange. Mosul was a sprawling city of about 2.5 million people in northern Iraq. It was situated right along the Tigris River and had been strategically important to Saddam Hussein because of its location close to the Kurdish territories. The other major thing I knew about Mosul was that Saddam's two sons, Uday and Qusay, a couple of really, really evil dudes, had been killed there early in the war in 2003.

The 101st Airborne had set up operations there and the Battle of Mosul was won in November of 2004, but at a pretty high cost. A lot of the Iraqi security forces fighting on our side left the area. It was hard to blame them. The insurgents had come in and let loose with a series of attacks against the police and security forces. They weren't the only ones who left. About a half million or so other Iraqis got the hell out of there because things were so unsafe.

Without those security groups in place, the city was left in chaos for a while. With no homegrown security forces, and with infrastructure and things like power plants being severely damaged, it was a bit of a Wild West town, with the bad guys running loose. We were there to try to keep control and help with the rebuilding efforts; but we'd been trained to fight battles, and this transitioning into the roles of peacekeepers and rebuilders wasn't what most of us had signed up for.

We were in country less than eight hours when we were sent out to do a bit of recon in the area. I was thinking of it as a tour of the city to help us get a sense of what was where more than any kind of really detailed exploration or intelligence gathering. Because the regular Army forces were on rotations that lasted anywhere from a year to a year and a half instead of the 90 to 120 days our Special Operations units were doing, and none of us had been in Mosul before, we hooked up with a guy from the 101st Airborne to be our tour leader.

Keith was a good guy, a gangly blond with a horsey grin who was really amped up to be working with us. I can still picture him coming up to us, his feet wide and his hips thrust forward, looking like he'd just gotten off a horse a few seconds earlier.

"Well, all right then. Rangers need some showing around. I'm down with that."

He stuck his hand out and I shook it, noticing how bony it was and how pale it was compared to his deeply tanned face. He took off his Oakley sunglasses to look me in the eye, and I could see the faint lines where the glasses' temples had blocked the sun, giving his face a kind of war-paint look.

I was still so new that I didn't think much about how I was a Ranger and he was just a regular grunt. I was on his territory and wanted to learn about the best routes through the city and what we were supposed to be on the alert for and where. I didn't say anything to him like this, but I was really pretty concerned about—okay, scared of—improvised explosive devices (IEDs).

By that time, probably everybody in the States and definitely everybody in the military knew about this tactic that the insurgents employed. They'd taken the old idea of mines—their use goes back centuries and centuries to when gunpowder was first developed—where you'd have to come in contact with a pressure plate or some other device to detonate an explosive charge. Those kinds of things were manufactured in mass quantities back in the day and were planted in the ground in big numbers in certain locations to keep infantry and vehicles from getting though.

An IED has five components: a switch (activator), an initiator (fuse), a container (body), a charge (explosive), and a power source (battery). What the Haji—a term we used for any of the various factions we fought against—

had figured out was how to set them off in sophisticated ways that didn't require coming in contact with them. They'd figured out ways to have them explode by remote control. That was scary to me in a way that a more passive land mine wasn't. Just the idea that some kind of sophisticated electronics were involved made them feel more deadly, maybe because I grew up in an age when electronics and technology had become so advanced it was hard to understand how things worked. I guess we fear more what we don't understand.

Eight hours into my time in country, I was at the controls of a Stryker following our tour guide. Richie, a guy who was just a couple of months ahead of me in Ranger School, was the tank commander (TC). We had about the same amount of experience, so Richie was always pretty cool in dealing with me as equals. Because you don't drive a Stryker by looking out a view port or window, the TC and the driver have to coordinate their efforts. I was looking at the little 10-by-12-inch screen, which really only gave me a view of what was directly ahead of me maybe ten feet or so, while listening to Richie guide me through a series of right- and left-hand turns.

We were in an older part of Mosul and the streets were so narrow I couldn't believe that they were designated as two-way streets. The Stryker barely fit in between the cars parked haphazardly along each side of the road. At one point, I popped open the hatch to get a wider view. The rest of the guys—there were three of them in addition to Richie—were all hanging out of their ports in the back. We weren't on a formal operation, so we felt comfortable being exposed like we were.

Our guide, Sergeant Davis, was calmly narrating for us, and his voice had started to become white noise, like the sound of the engine and the tires crunching over rocks and bricks, debris from the bombing we'd done there.

"We're going to make a left here onto a route designated Chicago, but what we call RPG Alley."

That got my attention. I felt a quick flutter in my gut as RPGs—rocket-propelled grenades—got added to my list alongside IEDs. I turtled my head closer to my shoulders and felt my helmet drop lower over my night vision goggles, suddenly immersing me in darkness. A few seconds later, I adjusted everything and I had to squint to make out anything beyond the greenish glare flaring from glass on the road and from the parked vehicles. My eyes climbed the walls of the buildings, using the pockmarks from shrapnel as visual footholds.

What had left those marks?

I scanned the rooftops. In my mind's eye I saw, from that heightened perspective, an RPG like a hard-thrown but wobbly football coming right at us.

At that point, I felt my knees go a little weak and I started to bounce my legs a bit with nervous anxiety.

"We're going to make a left again and then another left and head back in," Davis said, his voice again soothing and practiced, like a tour operator in Chicago pointing kind of horrible camouflage. I couldn't see any of the guys in Keith's Stryker moving around outside the vehicle. A terrible thought hit me. What if its fuel tank had ignited, and with all the electronics down and the hatches inoperable those guys were trapped in there? How frigging awful would it be to get incinerated inside that thing?

Fortunately, the emergency hatch had a mechanical release, and I saw some of the guys spilling out the back of it. We'd trained for those kinds of exits. The guys were moving quickly, but they didn't look panicked.

Over the sounds of my thoughts and the clamor inside our rig, I could hear Keith yelling, his voice high-pitched and rapid, "I'm hit. I'm hit. My leg. I think it's fucked up. It might be gone. Holy shit."

I watched as a guy from our unit named Lash, one of the really balls-out assaulters, clambered onto the top of the Stryker. He knelt down and started yanking at the hatch above the operator's position. Finally, he got it open and then reached down with one arm like he's sticking it down a storm drain, and I saw his white teeth through the swirling smoke. A few seconds later, Keith's helmet came out, and it was bobbing around while Keith was still yelling that's he's been hit. In a way, it was like I was watching some kind of bizarre birth scene. Lash reached in again, this time with both hands with his legs spread and his feet on the rim of the opening for leverage. He leaned back and heaved, and Keith emerged, bloody and screaming.

out the city's architectural highlights. "This is the easy route back. Been down this way a bunch of times. Nothing ever goes on. The people along here seem friendlier than a lot of other folks. Not sure why, but we get a few smiles and waves and nods."

I settled back down inside the Stryker and gunned the throttle to keep our spacing. We were moving pretty good, rumbling along at about thirty-five miles an hour. The Stryker's chassis was sending pleasant vibrations up through my boots, a gentle kind of massage.

A few seconds later, the lead Stryker, carrying our tour guide and piloted by Keith, was suddenly engulfed in a plume of black smoke rising up out of the ground. A moment after I saw that on the screen, I could feel the concussion wave knocking my head from side to side like I was a bobblehead doll wobbling before it stilled.

"IED. IED. IED," I screamed over the comms while simultaneously thinking, "WTF could have lifted that Stryker off the ground like that?"

I didn't have much time to think of an answer. I immediately went into autopilot; we'd trained and trained for situations just like this one. I throttled up and maneuvered alongside the damaged vehicle, Richie's instructions barely registering in my mind. I popped back up into the open air, the smell of burning rubber and super-heated metal stinging my throat and nose. I could barely see through the smoke, but I could make out the sides of the Stryker, streaked with oil and singe marks like some

While I was watching this, I reached down and pulled out my M4. I was hoping that I'd spot somebody with a weapon, some bad guy who I could take out all of my anger on. I figured that somebody nearby had called in our position and had that device detonated.

A couple of medics swarmed all over Keith, lowering him to the heaved-up pavement. They cut off his pants. I watched as Keith tried to keep his junk covered up, not wanting to expose himself to everyone as he's being carried to the medical Stryker. His eyes were slammed shut and it looked like someone was pulling all the skin of his face tight and tying it into a kind of bun.

As soon as he was loaded in, the Stryker took off.

We all formed a defensive perimeter around the vehicle. A couple of mechanics came up and assessed the damage. The last thing we wanted was for any of the bad guys to get ahold of our equipment. The guys aboard it had done their job immediately. They'd secured any sensitive documents and electronics they could carry out with them. Next we faced a decision: to call in a 500-pound bomb to destroy the Stryker completely to keep the enemy from getting ahold of it, or to salvage the thing and get it towed out of there. We decided to go for the second option.

As we stood around waiting, I talked to one of the mechanics.

"Lucky," he said, and then thought about that statement. "Hard to use that word, but it's true. The dumb fuck who planted the thing went too deep. Another six inches, a foot closer to the surface, would have split that Stryker open like a can of beans."

I didn't want to think what that would have meant for the guys inside. I could tell the mechanic didn't either.

"Glad to be a Ranger," he said, a mix of a question and a statement.

"Roger that," I told him.

I knew that he was referring to our equipment. Once again, being with a Spec Ops unit had paid off. Our Strykers were more heavily armored than the standard-issue ones were. For whatever reason, our budgets were much higher than the regular Army's. Didn't really seem fair, but I knew that if I was to ask Keith what he thought about "fair," he'd have a hard time seeing it any other way than this: He got out of it alive and essentially intact and that was all that mattered. Questions of budgets and whys were above his pay grade.

Later, we'd learn that Keith had a fractured tibia and some lacerations. He returned to his unit within a month and a half, and would eventually be awarded the Purple Heart.

I can't say for sure what happened to the Stryker, but for all my fears about IEDs, seeing firsthand how that one stood up to what was a substantial blast gave me a lot more confidence. The insurgents could dish it out, but we were adapting and proving that we could take it.

In the immediate, though, I was scared shitless. First

day in, traveling down a road that was supposed to be no problem and an IED doing that to us? What was in store for us the rest of the way in Mosul?

Shortly after Keith returned following his rehab, we got approached by a commander from the 101st Airborne. Even though for security reasons we didn't have any kind of markings on our uniforms, he knew that we were likely Spec Ops. Privately, I kind of got off on the idea that some guys might have thought we were CIA or NSA, since all those agency guys were similarly unmarked, but I was never really comfortable with the idea that rank, individual or group, came with privileges. I was grateful that we had the best kit and the best, most armored Strykers, but that didn't mean that I was going to flaunt any of that. That also doesn't mean that I wasn't proud to be a Ranger—far from it. I liked the idea that other units looked up to us and that from time to time we could lend them a hand. That was all a part of leading the way. These guys needed us, and we were glad to help them out.

In early 2007, not only were some of the other regular Army units laboring under the handicap of not having the best equipment, but the rules of engagement (ROEs), which seemed to be constantly changing, had them kind of hamstrung. That's why this commander came to us to ask for our help. Rules of engagement are a necessary part of warfare, but you ask any guys who served in Iraq and Afghanistan during this period and they'll likely tell you—as would guys who fought in Vietnam and likely every other conflict we've been involved in as a country—that our respect for and implementation of ROEs was far more strict and far more restrictive than what the bad guys had in place. Look at it this way: We weren't beheading people, burning up bodies and hanging them in public places, or doing anything remotely barbaric.

The problem this commander was facing was kind of simple. By the time he approached us in 2007, the ROEs had changed to the point that even when his guys were under attack, they weren't allowed to return fire. In particular, this happened every time they passed a particular hotel in Mosul. All they could do was to drive past the area as quick as they could to avoid taking too many hits. They were motoring along a major thoroughfare that was a regular "secured" route. Because we were Rangers, we operated under a different set of ROEs. We could, and took every legitimate opportunity to, return fire.

We were so eager to help out that we didn't ask too many questions about why the commander felt like this was the best solution. I wasn't about to ask, since it seemed like this was a chance for me to get some real action under my belt. Despite how I felt about IEDs and the threat they posed, I was still itching to see some real combat. See, I didn't mind the idea of facing a real enemy fair and square. I didn't like the idea of some Haji sneaking around at night planting IEDs and then some other bad dudes sitting there in the safety of some room pressing a button or whatever to try to blow us up. I know that all is fair in love and war and all that, but to me that's just a saying, not a way human beings ought to behave.

I'd read a lot about war as a kid and I once came across a book about a special unit that the Army developed in World War II. They recruited a bunch of actors, artists, and others who practiced deceptive tactics—forging documents, using fake balloon tanks and various equipment to fool the enemy into thinking we had taken positions we hadn't, and perpetrating all kinds of other trickery. So when the commander suggested that we "pretend" to be like his regular Army unit, I was all for that. We'd wear uniforms like theirs, put on their regimental patches, and drive by that hotel and give those bad guys all kinds of hell.

We had downtime during the day, so we could fit the operation, which we called the Hotel Party, into our schedule. This would be a daytime operation, and we normally operated at night.

Just before we set out, Bill Youngman, one of the other Stryker drivers like me and a member of the weapons squad, said, "I don't know about this. It's pretty cool and all that we're going to be able to do this, but we're Stryker drivers. We haven't trained for this kind of thing."

"Are you kidding me?" Hogan said, his voice a kind of hacking cough that reminded me of a dog trying to get a hair out of its throat. "What's to train for? Drive.

Shoot. Hell, fucking gangbangers do this kind of thing all the time."

We all laughed a bit at that.

I sat there fitting a mini-scope to my M4.

Using my nickname, Hogan said, "Look at Irv, dude. He's into it. Like being back in the 'hood, right?"

I let that pass. I didn't know what kind of a 'hood he thought I came from, but the only things I ever shot in my 'hood were a bird and a window, and I felt guilty about both for weeks after. I wasn't feeling guilty about the possibility of shooting a bad guy in Iraq, though. In a way the scope was kind of ridiculous, but I was still fascinated with sniping and all that went into it, and if I could use that scope and my M4 to get some feel for what it was like to take aim and take out a guy at six or eight hundred meters, then I was going to do it. And I wasn't going to care what anybody else said or thought.

We finished kitting up and I climbed behind the controls of the Stryker, my heart beating at a rate nearly as fast as the pistons pounding in that Caterpillar diesel engine. I grabbed my M4 and put it in what I called the abyss—this space right next to the operator's seat that was a deep and dark-seeming black hole. Anything smaller than an M4 put in it would just get swallowed up, never to be seen again. Our platoon leader, Richie, shook his head when he saw me stowing my weapon there. He added his M4.

"I'm not even going to ask where you got that scope

from," he said. He paused and a second later said, "That's badass, Irv. Good thinking."

Just like the video displays we had to watch when we drove the Strykers offered us just a limited view of our surroundings, the same had been true of our night vision. Going out into the streets of Mosul in full-on daylight was literally and figuratively eye-opening. I'd heard people say that we should blow the Iraqis and others into the Stone Age, and it kind of looked like we had tried. Shattered buildings and islands of rubble all dotted the landscape, things that I hadn't been able to see when I was caught up in the visual tight close-up of our operations. I was reminded of the photos I'd seen of American cities in the '60s when riots tore through places like Detroit and other urban areas.

As we approached the building that the commander had told us about, I could see that it was about ten stories tall and stretched along for nearly half a block. And just as we'd been told, as soon as we were within a few hundred yards, I heard small-arms rounds plinking off our armor. I was driving the lead vehicle and before I could report the enemy contact, I heard the other drivers chiming in.

"Fuckin' bastards," I heard Keith say. He was no longer a driver since the IED incident. His leg was better, but he'd come back and taken on a role as a .50-cal gunner, utilizing its remote control operation with great accuracy.

As we drew even with the building, I braked hard and brought us to a quick stop. That had to confuse the snipers. The regular Army guys would just have hauled ass in their Humvees instead of staying put like we were. We were much more protected in the Stryker and wanted to take those guys out in the worst way.

We took a beat and assessed the situation. I grabbed my M4, and while I was doing that, I could hear the RWS (remote weapon station) guns—the .50-cal machine guns—swiveling to our right. There must have been fifty or more windows facing the street in that building and, from the sound of things, an insurgent was in every one of them. What was funny was that as the guns were pivoting on the enemy position, the plinking and reports from the Hajis' weapons went quiet. I could imagine all of them looking out at us and in unison saying their version of "Holy shit" as they realized what was about to happen. It was almost like I could hear the collective sound of a hundred or more assholes puckering simultaneously.

In the next instant, the .50-caliber guns started spitting fire at them. Instead of that plinking sound, I heard the spent casings of the .50-cals rattling around, and I smelled the chemical odor of our weapons discharging. I guess the bad guys had time to recover, because in the next moments we started to take really heavy fire. I don't know why I did this, but I had lit up a cigarette like some stupid punk thinking he's in a movie and squinting past the smoke down the barrel of his rifle. I popped open my hatch and looked through the scope to see what was going on. I caught a glimpse of a group of our assaulters busting across the short gap between the Strykers and the building, maybe three hundred yards at the most. They were bent on doing a room clearing. I was thinking that there were way too many rooms and way too many bad guys, but there they were. I was always amazed by how efficient these guys were when clearing rooms, but I figured there were at least a hundred rooms and that was going to take a couple of hours at least—especially since there seemed to be targets in every room.

"Suppressive fire! Suppressive fire!" I heard their team leader yelling over the comms.

I heard the report of multiple .50-cal machine guns going off. Then I heard Keith firing words as fast as rounds.

"It's gone. It's gone. Mother—" The .50-cal was normally pretty reliable, but ours had gone down. I grabbed the M4 and scrambled out of the hatch. I took a spread-eagle position behind the .50-cal's mounting platform. I squinted through the scope and fanned along a line of windows, looking for any kind of movement. A couple of times, I saw a head moving or the muzzle of an AK waggling around the corner of an opening, and I squeezed off a few rounds, but every one of them missed. I held focus on a position I'd fired on and saw a puff of smoke coming from the stone façade of the building. I fired again and got the same result—too low!

"Aww, crap!" I muttered, and shook my head at my stupidity.

"Hold up, dumb shit," I told myself.

I aimed again, this time holding the rifle so the number 3 hash mark in the ACOG scope was centered right on a bad guy's head. I squeezed the trigger and then watched as the dude dropped out of sight below the window ledge.

It took a moment for it to sink in. I'd just shot somebody in the head. I was pumped, but I knew that I had to relax a bit; too much adrenaline would make it hard for me to stay focused. I aimed again on that same window, because I saw another shape in it. I fired. Same result. Another one dropped. I blinked; it was like I was playing whack-a-mole or something. Another dude popped up. Was it the first guy that I thought I'd taken out? Were there a bunch of dudes in that room?

Didn't matter. I needed to take them out even if they seemed like they were zombies or something.

The firefight went on like that for what seemed to be hours. I was changing mags while a couple of other guys were working to repair the .50-cal. Richie was up there with two other guys and the next thing I know, I see him standing behind the .50-cal. He was tearing at the pins that held it on its stand. In a few seconds he had it loose, and instead of firing it from the safety of the cabin using the remote control functions, he started to free-gun it. I couldn't tell if it was a snarl or a smile or a little of both that lit up his face, but he was bouncing a bit with the recoil and the weight of the gun as he manually operated it.

A few seconds later, one of the bad guys fired a shot that hit inside the ammo can that held the .50-cal rounds. The can jumped with the explosion and I kept thinking all hell could break loose if that set off a chain reaction. Richie looked down at the can, frowning and shaking his head but still letting loose with the machine gun.

"Where's the new guy?" he shouted above the din of discharging weapons.

For a second I was confused. I could barely hear Richie, and then I remembered that we'd had a newbie join us for a ride-along—kind of like what I'd been through when I was first downrange.

I pointed down the hatch into the cabin. A second later, another round from one of the Hajis' AKs struck the ammo can again. I watched fascinated as a single .50-cal round spun up out of the can like a fish going after a fly, then disappeared beneath the surface into the cabin. I cringed and waited, but heard nothing.

"Tell that asshole to get the fuck up here. I need help loading!" Richie screamed.

I peered inside the cabin. The new guy sat crouched with his back pressed against the rear bulkhead of the vehicle. His eyes were wide as grapes and he sat there with his hands pressed against his ears.

"Dude, we're losing fire superiority. We need you."

I wasn't sure if the cherry new guy didn't hear me or if he didn't care. I was pretty pissed off at that point. We thought we were going out for a kind of joyride to take care of some punks that were messing with our little brothers, but now we were engaged in a serious battle and this shithead wasn't doing a damn thing to help us out.

I screamed at him, calling him every name in the book, but he just sat there cringing.

Fuck this, I thought, I don't have time to convince this dude to do his job. I got back on the deck and resumed firing. Richie looked over at me and set the weapon down for a second and stood there with his hands at his sides, his palms forward, shrugging his shoulders as if to say, "What's up?"

"He's freaking out," I said between pulls of the trigger. "He's down there sitting in a puddle of his own piss."

In the middle of all this chaotic action, Richie stood there for another second, looked skyward, then raised his arms up like he was asking the gods for an answer as to why this new guy was down there while the rest of us were up there getting our asses fired at. He dropped to his knees and peered into the cabin. He pulled his head out and started laughing, raising and lowering a closed fist in man-code for a guy beating off.

Enough said. We didn't have time for any more attempts to get our "reinforcement" off his ass.

I resumed firing as quickly as I could and was growing

frustrated with my inaccuracy and the seemingly endless supply of bad guys popping up in the same window.

After a while, I heard the distinctive thumping of a chopper's rotors and out of the corner of my eye saw the fish-head shape and eyes of an OH-58 Kiowa helicopter coming in on the attack. Above it was another chopper and above that one, with maybe two hundred feet of elevation distance separating it from the rest of the school, was a third. They took turns coming on a shallow dive to fire rockets and their machine gun rounds at the hotel. It was like this big three-pedaled elliptical machine rising and falling, coming forward and falling back in a kind of brutal ballet. I had to take my eyes off it and concentrate on my job, but man, those dudes could handle those machines.

I got a little worried because at one point, one of the OH-58s came in and must have hit a pocket of turbulence caused by the concussive effects of the rocket explosion and lost altitude, dipping way down to maybe twenty feet off the ground before the pilot saved it and gained airspeed and climbed steeply and banked sharply to get to the top of the ride, then hovered there. A few moments later, another chopper came in and experienced a similar kind of flutter in flight path. A rocket flared off its flanks, and I knew that something wasn't right. I'd seen laser-guided missiles before, and they don't always travel in a straight line; instead, they veer from side to side and take a funky route to their target. This wasn't like that, though. This was a straight shot and seemed to be coming right at us at about a 25-degree angle.

Those missiles haul ass. I didn't even have time to scream; I watched it as it hit the pavement maybe fifteen yards from the left front quarter panel of our Stryker. I heard it plink as it struck the ground, watched sparks splay off its flanks as metal hit asphalt, and then felt my jaw drop and my balls contract as that missile skipped off the ground and into the air before it exploded halfway between our position and the hotel. Its fireworks display may as well have spelled out, "Today is your lucky day!"

Richie and I exchanged dumbfounded looks before getting back to firing our weapons. Next thing I know, I hear over the comms that some of the teams are going black on ammo—running out. The assault team was still trying to close the gap between our position and the building.

"Bounding back! Bounding back!" I heard them say.

I laid down cover fire yards in front of them. For some reason, one of the Hajis came out of a sliding door on the ground floor and I took him out, wondering for a minute how many of them I'd killed that day.

It's weird the kind of things you remember from these firefights that go on for hours, but at one point I became fixated on an assault gunner by the name of Davis. Maybe it's because I'm so short, but it seemed like Davis was a giant of a guy, six-five or so, so tall that his military-issue stuff never seemed to fit him right. I saw him behind a little rock, a whole lot of his body sticking out around it, but a rock big enough that I could have been completely hidden. He darted from there, moving with the kind of quickness you wouldn't expect from a guy that size, kind of like Rob Gronkowski of the Patriots sneaking out from the offensive line and settling into a little zone. Only Davis wasn't behind the D-line and the linebackers, he was settled in behind a rectangular utility box out in front of the building.

He was to my right and I kind of saw him in a full side view, and I saw this splash of spray come out behind him. I thought, "Man, that was a huge sneeze, even for a big guy like that." He rocked back on his heels and then lurched forward a bit, his helmet going from a twelve to two and then to ten o'clock. I resumed firing and took my eye off of him for a few seconds. I returned my gaze to his position and I could see that something had changed. He was in direct sunlight and yet his back seemed to be in shadow. He was still firing his weapon, and then I watched him testing his shoulder, moving it around like a football player does when he's trying to get his shoulder pads back in position after taking a big hit.

Then I heard him over the comms.

"Hey, Platoon Sergeant Gritzer. I think I may be hit. A rock or something." Davis had this thick Southern accent. He's a gentleman country boy from the Deep South, very quiet and respectful and despite what he's reporting on, he sounds like he's ordering biscuits and gravy or something from a waitress who reminds him of his mom.

A second later, he added, "Aw! Dang it. I am hit."

I couldn't believe it, but he stood straight up, all six-foot-five of him, and he's now exposed three quarters of his body above that utility box. There's not a lot I could do but hope and pray for the guy and keep firing, so I did all of those.

Out of the corner of my eye, Doc Daniels was flying toward Davis. He grabbed him around the waist and it was like a little bitty defensive back trying to take down Gronk. Davis would not go down. Doc was too short to get up high enough to yank the big guy's shoulders and head and he's hopping and leaping, but Davis was still more or less upright. Doc must have got ahold of the quick release on Davis's body armor, because that clattered to the ground.

As I'm watching all that take place, I could hear Davis; he's madder than hell. I'd never heard him curse before but he was spewing quite a few of them.

"Son of a bitch shot me!" he screamed.

"Get down!"

"Gonna be hell to pay!"

"Get down!"

From my position I could see a large hole below Davis's shoulder blade and blood dripping down his back. We could hear everything over the comms and

Doc was asking for the medical Stryker to get there ASAP and for a quick extraction. "ASAP! ASAP!" I kept hearing those words over and over.

Doc was trying to calmly explain to Davis what was going on. He was afraid that the bullet had come in on such an angle that it snuck in beneath his body armor at shoulder level and exited about three quarters of the way down his back. Doc was concerned that Davis had gotten his lung punctured.

"Gimme a lollipop, Doc," Davis said, referring to the morphine doses that could be taken orally.

"Nope. Not in this case. Can't do that."

"C'mon. I just want a taste of one." Davis was pretty near to giggling by this point.

"I think you're going into shock; just lie still. We'll get some fluids into you."

"Naw, I'm not in shock. I'm just messin' with you. Doesn't hurt at all."

"Well, it's about to," Doc said.

Doc helped hustle him out of there, and as I watched Davis ducking into the Stryker, I heard some not so good news over the comms: "We're completely black on ammo. Repeat. Completely black," the chopper pilots reported.

No rockets.

No machine gun rounds.

No air support.

That last one wasn't true. The pilots did something I'd never seen. While still in control of their aircraft the pilots and the copilots flew in again, hanging out of the cockpit while firing their small arms at the targets, doing flyby after flyby until the ammo was depleted and we'd all managed to return to our Strykers.

As we fired up the engines, I heard the call to go in for an air strike, a 500-pounder. A few minutes later, we heard that payload being delivered from an F-16.

As we pulled into our FOB—our forward operating base—we were all still eager, with the exception of the new guy, to get back out there. We piled out of the Stryker and headed toward our compound so we could refit. The regular Army commander was there. He'd been monitoring things on the radios and he was yelling at us, "Stop. Stop. I want to talk to you guys."

We rushed past him into our ready room, grabbing C-4 explosive, grenades, and ammo, stuffing as much in as many places as we could. We didn't get out of there. The commander stood his ground, holding up his hands and telling us, "You're done!"

We had to accept that, but that didn't mean that we had to be happy about it. For a few days after, most of us involved in the Hotel Party walked around like we had a really bad hangover, mumbling our regrets but still kind of amped up by what we'd been through and the memories of the crazy shit that went down.

The next day, I called my mom and dad, but I didn't get into a whole lot of detail about what I'd just been through. As I was talking to them, I saw Davis walk in.

His arm was in a sling, but he didn't seem much the worse for wear, all things considered.

At first I wondered if something was wrong with him, because he was normally so soft-spoken but now he was practically shouting. Then I figured out what was up.

"Grandma! Grandma! I'm sorry, ma'am. I know you told me not to get shot."

A long pause followed.

"Yes, ma'am, I know that I need to listen to you. I know you've got more sense than me, Grandma." He stood there squinting hard and focusing on her words, then said, "You sure can count on that. I promise I won't get shot again."

We gave Davis all kinds of crap for that conversation with his "kinfolk," but we were glad that within a week or so he was back in action with us. He was really fortunate that the bullet passed straight through him. A deflection of a fraction of an inch to the left or right and it would have hit his lungs or some other vital organ, his spinal column.

Not something you want to think about for too long. Just give thanks and move on.

The good news was, as our deployment went on, we didn't hear of any more reports of anybody encountering trouble along that route. As a guy on the ground, it was hard for me to understand how somebody back in the safety of their office in the Pentagon could have decided that in our desire to bring the war in Iraq to an end we should take away an Army division's ability to defend itself.

That was the first time I'd seen one of our guys get wounded, and it shook me up. I was also kind of confused from that point forward about just what our role was there. Not our role as a Spec Ops unit—that was clear to me. What was strange was that during the day, with our government's decision to close down the war, we had the regular Army guys out there helping to build schools, make a public presence, build a democracy, and all of that. But when the sun went down, we were out on those same streets, taking out targets, trying to rid the country of al-Qaeda big shots. I couldn't quite grasp the big picture.

Not too long ago, I heard that Mosul had fallen under the control of ISIL, ISIS, or the IS or whatever we are referring to those jokers as these days. We didn't lose anybody during the Hotel Party operation, but I knew that the regular Army units had suffered a few casualties and fatalities along that corridor. At the time I didn't think too much about all of that. We'd picked up a mission, helped some guys out, got back, and restocked and refocused the next day thinking that we'd done a good job, done what was asked of us. I wish that I could look at things that simply today.

All I know is that we had each other's backs at the time and did everything we could to support one another. Whether or not the higher-ups did the same is tough to say. I wasn't being paid to make all those kinds of high-level decisions about rules of engagement; I was there to make sure that all my brothers got back inside the wire safe and sound. All else aside, that was my job, and the longer I was out there, the more evidence I saw that the rest of the guys felt much the same way. We didn't need any PowerPoint presentations to spell that out for us. We lived and breathed it every day, and seeing it in action and feeling it to my core was a wonderful thing. All I could hope for the new guy who bailed on us was that he'd learned something from seeing how the rest of the guys manned up and did their jobs.

TWO

THINK FIRST, ASK QUESTIONS, AND THEN FIRE

WHEN THE WOOD pallets come out, it's pretty easy for everybody to load up your situational awareness along with all the rest of your gear. You're ready for home at the end of your four months, and a certain level of chill settles in when the order comes down for you to start packing up and piling your gear on the pallets for the airlift to take you from downrange to down home.

That was the combination relaxed and anticipatory state of mind most of the guys and me in the 3rd Ranger Battalion were in during the last week of July 2006. It's hard to think of anything being "chill" when it's 100-plus degrees every day. I have to admit I was probably less chill than some of the others. I was the cherry new guy, this being my first deployment, after all. A little of the "Wow, I'm actually out here doing this stuff" had been sweated out of me, but, at eighteen years old, I was still pretty thrilled to be out there as a gunner, toting my Mark 48 machine gun into approximately 120 operations during that deployment. Truth was, though, I spent much more of my time inside the Stryker, kind of acting as a chauffeur delivering and returning the other team members.

Still, that's a lot of hours spent outside the wire, but to that point, within hours of heading for home, I'd never come under enemy fire. I was almost to the point that on some subconscious level, I believed the enemy wasn't capable of firing back. That may sound incredibly naïve of me, but unless you've been through what we did, it's easy to say what we *should have been* prepared for. I'm not making excuses, but in all my training, nobody had ever fired live rounds at me. In so many of my earliest operations during that first deployment, we so outmanned and outgunned the enemy that it really didn't seem like we were in that much danger.

As eager as I was to see combat and to see what I was made of, I had to learn one of the most fundamental lessons of all before I could truly become a soldier. I had to learn to think before I shot. Sounds simple, but as the rules of engagement evolved and the firefights and the sniper operations and opportunities became more and more complicated, that simplest of rules took on more dimensions than I had ever thought possible.

I've heard the expression "Baptism by Fire" to describe getting thrown into the middle of a tough situation when you're just starting out, but what I remember more is the "Baptism by Flood" that happened just days before we started to pack up all our extra kit. We'd been out on an operation and came back to find our compound under four feet of water. Fortunately, our Containerized Housing Unit (CHU) was mostly watertight, so not a lot of moisture seeped into our quarters. Funny thing was, nobody ever explained to us how all that water got in there, if a levee or a dam broke somewhere. Weird to be in the middle of so much heat and dust and desertlike conditions and then to be wading through waist-deep water.

The pallets came out after the waters receded, but every CHU and other building on the compound was left with a kind of whitish-green ring around it.

Just hours before our scheduled departure stateside, I was standing there with a couple of guys talking about that ring and how weird that whole flooding episode was. Just then, the chirp of all our pagers going off, sounding like a flock of birds waking in the morning, cut that discussion short.

"Naw, naw!"

I looked over at another machine gunner, Johnson, a good dude from South Florida.

He shook his head ferociously and bent at the waist, adding, "Can't be. Not today." He punched his thigh and looked skyward.

"Maybe they're just testing them out," Ramirez said, his voice kind of cracking and rising like static when he said the word "out."

Our comms were always giving us trouble, so that seemed possible.

Our team leader, Lieutenant Chase, stood reading the code on his device, squinting in the bright sunlight and trying to shade the display. "This is no test, my friends. This is a TST."

Time Sensitive Target operation. So much for being able to take it easy before we headed home. It was going to be on, and we didn't have much time to think about home.

We had ten minutes to get our full battle rattle on. In an instant, guys are tearing into the bags piled on the pallets. Most of them hadn't kept it light, so they had to dig out their mission gear from bags where they'd also stowed all their personal stuff: DVD players, Xboxes, and what seemed like a whole Best Buy full of cables and adapters and whatnot. I didn't have all that stuff, so I grabbed my assault pack and eight hundred additional rounds of 7.62 ammunition to go with the two hundred in the Mark 48 and I was ready to roll. I jogged over to the Tactical Operations Center (TOC) before remembering that, with us just about to leave, all our intelligence equipment was packed up. I diverted to the temporary briefing room, a small hut really, and as I entered it, my team leader, Juan, grabbed me by the pack.

"Front row, Irving. This is important. Pay attention."

I didn't have time to think too much about why he was singling me out as a guy who needed to pay attention. A few seconds later, the commander walked in.

He rotated his head left and then right like he was cracking the bones in his neck to loosen them up. "I need you guys to get back into fight mode. I know that a lot of you were thinking we'd wrapped things up. We haven't."

He started the briefing, and as hard as it was for thirty-five guys to look at one thirty-or-so-inch screen to view the drone footage of the area and its terrain, we all leaned in and watched and listened. As usual, we were told we were going after a high-value target (HVT), and the rest of the details of what was being called Operation Chicken Coop were pretty straightforward. A helicopter drop-off, about five or six kilometers on foot, and then a target in the middle of a palm grove. The usual compound—a few squat buildings set around a central courtyard.

The next thing I knew, I was drifting off in the open doorway of a CH-47 Chinook, lulled to sleep by the drone of the engines and the fact that it was one o'clock in the morning. I was awakened by the two-minute alert. Then a minute later, I could feel the bladder-burning sensation of the chopper flaring up, slowing suddenly in anticipation of a landing. We came in really hot and bounced a few times before landing.

"Holy shit, dude," I thought. "Did you crash us?"

I'd never experienced anything like that before. I sat there for a second, stunned and feeling pain rising up from my lower back all along my spine to the top of my head. I wasn't the only one shaken up by the landing. I could hear all kinds of grunts or grumbles as we scrambled out the door and took up our security positions before watching the chopper take off.

We set out along a narrow path toward the little town of Baqubah. After about a half hour, I was regretting bringing so much ammo with me—those eight hundred rounds weighed more than fifty pounds. I couldn't shake off the fatigue I was feeling. All I wanted to do was just lie down someplace and rack out for hours and hours. I felt like my knee joints were melting like candle wax, and that with every step I was dripping nearer and nearer to the ground, like that pack was pile-driving me to the dirt.

I'd also loaded up my pack with about two gallons of water (nearly twenty more pounds), thinking it was better to be prepared for the worst than to be caught short. Thing was, I couldn't easily access the water from my pack. I was having a hard time staying awake. I was used to operating at night, but I hadn't had a thing to drink for hours and dehydration was making me drowsy. I was so relieved when we took a knee another half hour later, about five hundred yards from the objective.

My buddy Ramirez was right beside me.

"I'm dying, man," I said to him. "Can you help me out? Get my water?"

Ramirez rolled his eyes like I'd asked him to donate a kidney. A few seconds later, I felt him tugging at my pack, nearly dragging me down in his haste.

I emptied a liter down my throat in seconds. Just moments later, I could finally start to think straight.

"Suck it up and drive on," Ramirez said.

I nodded, "Roger that."

The assaulters, the snipers, and us in weapons all split up, according to the plan, disappearing into the dark and the brush. We low-crawled through a thicket of brambles, little spikes tearing at our skin and snagging our uniforms and gear. It was more irritating than painful, but enough to get me out of zombie mode. Nothing like a little bit of pain to pierce the fatigue.

We took up our positions. I saw a wall that reminded me of the biblical Wall of Jericho, though this one was only about eight feet tall. I couldn't figure out what it was for. Usually a wall or a fence is designed to keep something in or something out. This one just seemed to sit there dividing nothing from nothing.

We made sure our sectors of fire were good, and I

settled in, the smell of stagnant water like an ammonia capsule busted under my nose to keep me alert. I could faintly hear team leader Juan communicating with the assaulters. Up and to the north of me, I saw laser light as the two snipers, Alex and Matt, took up their positions. I didn't only have to raise my eye level to see them, I looked up to those guys in the other sense. They were both totally cool and put up with all my newbie and wannabe questions.

I thought back to one of my first operations as a gunner. I'd taken a position alongside a house. An instant later, I heard a pop and then a couple more. Above me, I heard the sound of glass shattering, and then a thump. Matt had taken out a hostile, the bullet traveling no more than a foot or so above my head. That got my attention, and I wanted to get some of what those sniper dudes were doing.

Instead, now, I was on the opposite end of what the enemy's snipers were doing. Ramirez and I were hunkered down, leaning against that wall. We heard a few pops and looked at one another. We had our sportings in—our ear protection—so everything was kind of muffled. A distant sound and then what felt like hail landing on our shoulders and pinging softly off our helmets. I looked up to the sky and could see the stars. No clouds, so no rain, no hail. What was going on?

Out of nowhere, I saw Juan half bent over, booking

it toward me. He horse-collar-tackled me and pressed my head into the dirt.

"Get your ass down! You're getting shot at!"

At first it didn't register. I'd thought the sound I heard was the low-level indicator for the batteries in my ear protection. That precipitation I'd thought I felt was bits of concrete and stone from the wall coming down on top of me. I lay there facedown for a few seconds, thinking, "Huh. So this is what it's like to be shot at. Never had this happen before."

Juan tapped my leg and pointed behind the wall. I scrambled around and we hunkered down there.

Next, I heard a series of controlled pairs—*boom-boom, boom-boom, boom-boom*—like the *lub-dub* of a heartbeat, and I knew that our guys were up on that rooftop taking dudes out. Then the sniper fire started to go and it sounded like all hell was breaking loose up on the roof of one of the buildings. I could picture the assault team up there firing down and the bad guys firing up at them, but at that point, I still hadn't seen a single enemy target. It was so strange to be there, like we were locked in a dark closet or something while, outside the house, war was going on.

Juan grabbed me and then Ramirez and led us to an intersection within this small compound. He positioned us there to contain another, smaller element that was in an adjacent building to where the main firefight was going on. Ramirez and I lay on the ground, forming a kind of V with our feet touching and our weapons balanced on their tripods, fanning out to give us the widest dispersal possible. We "talked" with our feet and our guns. If I saw something, I'd tap his boot. If he saw something, he'd do the same to mine. To that point, neither of us had fired our weapons. There was so much activity going on and everybody was so dangerously close that we didn't want to do any damage with friendly fire.

As I scanned the scene, I saw a little bird, one of our Army's MH-6 attack helicopters, issuing small rocket fire, going over a little grid of power lines and out into a field beyond the compound. That was oddly beautiful, the way it lit things up. I figured that Juan must have called them in. The thing hovered and kind of darted like a hummingbird. I watched as it spun around and headed away from our position, spun again on its horizontal axis, and came back in on another gun run. After it went past us, it was like somebody had grabbed it by its tail. The rotor still turned, but the engine sounded funny, and then it was like the body of the helicopter was one of those amusement park rides, the Tilt-a-Whirl, and the MH-6 spun around and around. By the sound of the motor winding up and down and then back up again, I could tell that the pilot was doing his best to gain control, but that didn't last for long. The helicopter kept spinning as it lost altitude. It had broken free of the power lines it had gotten snagged on and was about a mile beyond the compound when it crashed.

I felt this weird sensation coming up from my groin, like I'd just crested a hill going really fast in a car. This simple in-and-out operation we'd been sent on was now going to be a rescue. We'd all heard earlier about a downed pilot and crew from the 82nd Airborne who'd been captured. Some said they'd been beheaded; some said they'd been taken prisoner. Neither was a good option.

Out of the darkness, I saw Platoon Sergeant Salk, a hard-core Ranger who was the baddest dude I'd seen out there, running toward us, his helmet twisted to one side (as usual) and the muzzle of his gun still glowing. He looked like something out of a comic book or a video game, but he was one hard-charging Ranger and one of the best soldiers I'd ever seen.

"Ram, Irving," Salk shouted, "I need you two. Secure that crash site."

I nodded, but I was thinking, "Holy shit, you want the two of us to go with you?" That bird had traveled a considerable distance while trying to stay in the air. I still had about seventy-five pounds or more of ammo, water, and other gear in my pack, not to mention all my body armor. We'd be exposed most of the way out there. How fast could I run with all that on?

None of that mattered. We set out at a high pace, Salk urging us on, saying, "We're going to get there. Doesn't matter how far. We're there."

As we're running up and down a series of irrigation ditches, green tracer fire arced over us and I knew that it was enemy fire—our tracers were red. I puked in my mouth a bit from exertion and fear. This was the most hard-core action I'd ever seen. I kept hauling ass, knowing that I was running faster than I ever had during physical training without a pack or any other heavy gear on.

After getting through the series of irrigation ditches, we were up on a slight rise. To my right, I could see the shapes of other humans running alongside us, but slightly below our position, at a distance of two hundred yards. They were running along a road. I figured it was Haji, and I was thinking that I'd stop running and set up and light these dudes up. I stopped and took a second to let my vision clear. I saw that it was a few members of our assault team running alongside us and not the bad guys. I didn't have time to waste, so I took up running again, muttering "Thank God" under my breath. What if I'd opened fire on our own guys? I didn't want to think about it.

When we got near the crash site, Juan had caught up with us. He told me to take up a position on the perimeter.

"Nobody gets in. Nobody!"

His tone scared the shit out of me. He was shrieking and frantic.

Reports were coming in that nearly the entire population of the village of Baqubah was descending on our location.

I scanned the terrain and picked up sight of the pilot huddled in a semi-fetal position against a backdrop of reeds and weeds. His night vision was off, and I felt so bad for the guy. Sitting there in the pitch blackness had to be terrifying. All he had was a little MPF machine gun in his hand. He had like thirty rounds of 9-millimeter ammunition to defend himself with. Good luck with that.

I could see that the guy was much older than me, and it was weird to see how scared he was. I didn't blame him, but here I was, just a kid, really, and this grown man was on the ground rocking back and forth in terror.

I looked above him and I could see shadows and shapes coming in from behind him. All around me, I heard members of our various teams talking. Everyone was talking fast, moving fast, and there, out in the distance, kind of in freeze-frame, was this pilot. Over the sounds of our communications, I could hear the enemy shouting as they approached.

I'd seen the movie *Black Hawk Down;* I thought I was in my personal remake of it.

From overhead came the sound of approaching aircraft. I breathed a bit easier, but this was about to become a race—between us and the thirty-some bad guys—to the pilot.

Ramirez began firing blindly in the direction of the oncoming Hajis. Even with our night vision on, we would lose sight of them due to the rolling terrain. Then, with the AC-130 overhead, portions of the area were illuminated by the ship's spotlight. It was like him pointing out "they're here."

Here.

Here.

"Ram," as we usually called him, was going to town on those guys. I still hadn't fired, but lay there scanning the area. I admired how cool Ram was under pressure. He was a laid-back California dude from near San Francisco who could run like the wind; now he was laying down fire just like he was out on the range.

A few brief flashes of light caught my eye. Again, I felt like I was back in *Black Hawk Down,* remembering how the enemy had come in on a technical—a truck with a mounted machine gun in the bed. I figured that what I was now seeing, since it was coming from the same direction as the rest of the bad guys, had to be some heavily armed dudes who could probably wipe us all out if they got in the right position. It was my job to make sure they didn't get to that spot.

A few seconds later, I saw that it wasn't a technical. I saw something much worse: a tank. It was still only a few years since the war had really heated up, and at first I didn't take the time to think things through. To that point, I hadn't seen any of the Iraqis with a tank, but I was so naïve at that point that I figured a few of them must have survived the earlier battles and now here it was about to put a whipping on our asses. Along with the tank, there was a phalanx of infantry, walking alongside it.

I slid my weapon off safety and ran though the scenario in my head. Even though I've got the 48, we're all essentially there with small arms—especially compared to the tank. I was pretty sure that the rules of engagement gave me the right to open fire, but was that the right thing to do? Could I take a tank out? In all my training to that point, we hadn't covered this. I aimed my laser right into a port that I thought was where the operator of the armored vehicle was. I could see my light dancing a bit and I increased the amount of pressure on the trigger just a bit, thinking if I could put a good ten- or twenty-round burst in there, I'd be going a long way toward disabling that tank. I wanted a shot that was as good and clear as possible, so I kept repeating to myself, "Wait. Wait. Wait," as it drew nearer.

Then I looked around for a second and saw that the other Haji were getting even closer. Why weren't they with the tank? Why would they come at us in the open if they had that kind of firepower and protection? That made no sense, but they weren't a highly trained military, so maybe that explained everything.

I retargeted the tank; the guys alongside it must have spotted my laser, because they all ducked behind the massive machine. At least that made some sense to me. I took my finger off the trigger. I could feel that finger vibrating. I could have sworn that those dudes were wearing uniforms. Most of the insurgents I'd seen weren't dressed alike, as these guys were.

But what if they'd gotten ahold of some of our uniforms and were dressing up as us?

I was "what-if'ing" with every breath.

When I saw the turret swivel right toward my position, I made my choice. I was not going to fire. I could barely even swallow or breathe. A second later, Juan was at my side.

"Reinforcements. Awesome."

He could have been speaking some rare dialect of Russian. All the time I'd been deployed we'd never called in for any kind of backup. Why now? It made sense, though, with thirty-five of us against what seemed like hundreds of Hajis. We needed the help.

For the second time that night, I got away with something. I know the old saying about he who hesitates is lost, but in this case, I won because I didn't just go off and start firing. Some of the reason for that was discipline and training, some was fear, but a bit of confusion figured into it as well. I recalled playing games of HORSE back home with my buddies on the playground basketball courts. Sometimes it was better to be lucky than good, I remembered them saying. In this case, I was definitely "lucky," but I'd also done a "good" thing by having taken some time to think.

For most of that deployment I split my time between operations, pulling security with the gunner team and both driving and firing the 50-cal aboard the Stryker. I'd earned a reputation as a guy who was pretty fearless. I'd hard-charged that Stryker up and over things a number of times instead of trying to ease my way around obstacles. I'd done my fair share of firing that 50-cal, and wasn't trigger-happy or trigger-shy. I thought I was pretty comfortable in that environment, but on that night in July I had clearly showed my inexperience working in a hot zone with multiple firefights and other activity going on.

I got back to watching my sector. Ramirez was still firing away, and above that noise I could hear the AC-130s firing 105mm rounds and their distinctive three sounds: the firing, the sonic boom, and the impact. Those aircraft were thousands of feet in the sky and, like our guardian angels, were watching over us. While all that firepower was raining down, a Chinook came into view. It hovered over the downed little bird and I watched as cables were latched around the smaller helicopter; then the Chinook took off, just hauling ass out of there with that wounded chopper and its pilot now secure.

With that objective accomplished, I figured we might just be done for the night, but we weren't. As sometimes happened, intel that we gained in securing one objective led us right into another objective. These FRAGOs— fragmentary orders—weren't uncommon, but not having a full briefing in a TOC added to the tension that went along with doing something that seemed improvised instead of fully planned out. Given what had just happened—our operation transforming from a typical in-and-out into rescue and recovery—we were well prepared that night for anything at all to happen. That early in my career, though, I didn't like these follow-ons. They were always followed by another, and some-times another. It reminded me of being a kid out on errands with my mom. She'd tell me we were only going to this one place and then she'd stop at another and then another. When I had something in mind as having a specific beginning and end, I wanted to stick to the plan.

We set out on another 5K walk toward the new objec-tive. I was no longer tired, but wired. All the adrenaline was still feeding me and not tearing me down, but that didn't last the whole hike to the next town. For about the last click, or kilometer, I was back in bitching and moaning mentality. We weren't that far from where the firefight and chopper crash had occurred, so, of course, everybody in the village was up and about. That's not good. Who could you trust and who couldn't you trust? Basically you couldn't trust anyone, and that was un-nerving.

As we moved through the village's streets, Ramirez and I were instructed to split off and move down a series of side alleys and get ourselves parallel to the rest of the unit. I hated city fighting like this, because you had to keep your eyes ahead of you, to the side of you, and above you. Shots could come at you from any direction, including from behind you, and keeping your head on a swivel isn't easy. I knew that the snipers were above us, moving from rooftop to rooftop, and that gave me some comfort. I thought that would be cool as hell to be up there doing that. Also, they had the advantage of knowing that in nearly every case, there wouldn't be anyone up above them. I don't know what it was about knowing that somebody could be above me ready to fire down on me that was so spooky, but it was.

After advancing a few blocks, my worst fear was realized. I saw movement above me and to the right. I spotted a shadow moving and a balcony door catching a bit of light and then growing dark. A moment later, I could see the figure of a man standing on the balcony. He looked down at us and then leaned over the railing a bit, looking up and down the street. He went back inside. He came back a moment later, and I was shocked to see that he had brought a young boy out there with him. He kept the kid between himself and the railing, figuring that there was no way anyone would fire at him and risk hitting the kid. He was right. There was no way I was going to take that shot. The kid rose to just above the man's waist, so there was only a small opening to get at the guy. I could see that he was armed with an AK47, and that changed things a bit.

Juan said, "Hey, if he makes any kind of move you've got to take him."

I swallowed hard and said, "Okay. Roger that."

I hated being in that position, having to balance some kid's life in my hands and weighing it against the lives of our guys. Of course, I knew I had to do what was right. I was really pissed at that Iraqi man for using what was probably his kid as a human shield. What kind of person would do that?

I knew the chances of me firing off rounds to kill the adult and not hit the kid were very, very slim.

Still.

I took the weapon off safety and aimed it up at the guy. My hands felt like they were cramping, I was holding the gun so tight. My jaw ached with the tension and my finger was barely able to ease the trigger back. The 48 had a long pull, what felt like inches, and I kept easing it back. I was about halfway back with it when suddenly the guy on the balcony disappears from my vision. I heard a snap, followed by the AK clattering to the ground, followed by the sound of the guy landing in the street.

It took a second, but I realized that one of the snipers had taken out the bad dude. I eased back on the trigger and took in a deep gulp of air and exhaled slowly. I looked up at the balcony. The kid wasn't there anymore, but I knew that he hadn't been shot. I felt bad for the little dude having to see a guy I figured was his father or some other close relative getting shot.

Twenty yards ahead of me, the Muj lay sprawled on the ground. I walked up to him. He was the first kill that I saw up close. I wasn't grossed out by the sight of his deflated head or his twisted limbs. Anybody who'd put a kid in jeopardy like that deserved to die. I wondered briefly if maybe in that instant when he knew that he was hit he felt some kind of gratitude that he was taken out by a sniper and not by me or Ramirez with our 48s. Grateful not that he didn't experience any pain, but that he was the only one who got hit.

I couldn't think about that for too long—we still had an operation to conduct. But I kept coming back to that incident a long time after it ended. That kill shot had impressed me and left an impression on me. I wanted to become a sniper. I'd do a lot of reading about snipers in the years to come and eventually train to become one. I knew that some people had a problem with the ethics of sniping—that you hide out and kill somebody instead of facing them man-to-man. Well, tell me what was so manly and ethical about that bad dude on the balcony? In my mind, snipers save lives—our own and, in instances like this one, the life of an innocent little kid.

War meant killing, and in some people's minds no matter how it got done the taking of a life was either a good thing or a bad thing. What that sniper had done was definitely a good thing.

That whole night I was kind of lost in the fog of war, but as time went on, some things became much clearer while others would, no matter how hard I tried to focus on them, remain confusing and uncertain. I can see now that in a way, my desire to become a sniper was one way for me to lift myself up out of that fog of war. There was often so much going on around me during what should have been "easy" in-and-out operations that made up the bulk of what we were ordered to do that it took a kind of focus that maybe I didn't really have. I was fortunate that I hadn't made a rookie mistake on three occasions that night. I'd made the right decisions, and I was sure later on when I became a sniper that I'd made the right choice then, too. I had to experience a bit of war and get a feeling for what it was really all about before I could really understand all that went into thinking before you shoot.

THREE

THE VIRTUES OF PATIENCE

WHEN YOU'RE EIGHTEEN to twenty years old, you don't want to still hear about earning your stripes or that you have your whole life ahead of you so what's your hurry? You want what you want and you want it now. That's how I was when I was that age. In 2007, I'd been with the 3rd Ranger Battalion for more than two years. I have to admit that I was a bit impatient. I can't say that the novelty of driving a nearly twenty-ton Stryker armored vehicle had worn off. It was more like it had been sweated out of me. Climbing into that thing when it was 110 degrees outside was like being in a metal mobile oven. As the driver, I was separated from its 350-horsepower engine by a thin metal wall. More often than not, it seemed, the air-conditioning failed and I'd find myself drenched with perspiration after just a few minutes operating that thing outside the wire.

Despite all that, I had a love-hate relationship with the damn thing. When the call went out for us to load up and I'd twist those two knobs to get the Caterpillar engines to fire up, the throbbing of that beast was almost enough to take my mind off the fire it was producing behind me. The torque those things possessed was a wonder of physics and engineering. I was often the lead driver, and when daytime rolled around and we were headed back to base, I was like that proverbial horse that could smell the finish line. I wasn't going to let anything get in the way of me making it back there safely—even if the guys on the team riding on the back banged on the bulkhead and shouted at me to slow the hell down.

Now that enough time has lapsed that I can look back on things with a bit more maturity, I realize that I was so fortunate to be in Spec Ops when I was. In 2007 our budgets were, at least as far as I could tell, at an all-time high. Even the chow was something special—surf and turf Thursdays. Didn't get that kind of thing at home. We were on a rotation of ninety days in and ninety days out, and I was getting sent to all different kinds of schools. If I was of a different mind and moral set, I could have been set for a life of crime outside the military. I'd been taught how to hot-wire cars and break into buildings, and I'd acquired a whole bunch of other sets of skills that made me a jack-of-all-trades. That was important because as of 2007, I had four different job titles—Stryker driver, machine gun team leader, heavy weapons specialist, and designated marksman.

The last of those was the one that mattered the most to me. I know that a jack-of-all-trades isn't supposed to master any of his skills, but I have to say that I was pretty damn good with an M16A rifle with a scope on it. When I went to DDM school (to become a Designated Defensive Marksman), I was surprised to find out that we weren't going to be using sniper weapons systems— just the trusty old standard-issue M16A. Some of the first demonstrations I saw with that weapon were of guys firing at targets five hundred yards away. Damn impressive. Eventually during that training program, we'd stretch those weapons out to eight hundred yards while firing at human-silhouette targets with 77-grain hollowpoint .560 ammo. That feeling of power was almost as great as the one those Stryker motors produced.

The Army wanted us to be able to pick up the slack in case one of the snipers went down with a mechanical issue or got wounded. Here's where another kind of love-hate thing reared its ugly head. I would have loved to have been called on to use that training, but I hated thinking about the reason why I'd have that opportunity. Later on, when I became a sniper and talked with guys who hadn't been called on to use their skills, I could see some of the envy in their eyes. I was feeling that back in

2007 as my first deployment of that year was winding down to a close.

I also had a bit of a love-hate relationship with the schedule we were on. Sure, ninety days sometimes seemed like a long time, but it was also never enough time for me to see all the kinds of action that I wanted to. If I had all that training and all those skills, from breaching doors to driving Strykers to leading the machine gunners to having some long-range rifle abilities, I wanted to use them. It wasn't so much "use it or lose it"; it was more like I got all these cool toys at my disposal and the Army has invested so much time and money in training me, why can't they just let me loose to do my things?

It was like if my parents had sent me to high-performance-driving school, had given me a Porsche 911, and then had installed a governor on that car's motor that kept it from going more than sixty miles an hour. What was the point of all that? Worse, a lot of the time, I was simply a passenger in the car while one of my buddies or my parents were driving and having all the fun.

Ironically, with just twelve hours to go before we were to fly back home, we got briefed on a final mission that was, to my mind, all about frustration and futility. We were informed that an Iraqi prison break had occurred at a detention center under the Iraqis' "control." Most of the frustration was due to the fact that the first two years I'd spent in Iraq on my various deployments had been mostly about putting bad guys in these detention centers. I was pretty sure they wouldn't be rolling out any red carpets for us when we showed up. It didn't make much sense that one of them would recognize me individually, but still, as we sat in on the briefing, I started to get a bad feeling about how things might go down.

Also, I remembered watching TV back in the States when I was younger and seeing shows about what it was like inside America's prisons. It was chaotic at best, and a lot of those guys in there got to be a lot worse as human beings as a result of being put together with a bunch of other sociopaths. If these people in Iraq were killing each other with suicide bombings nearly every day, then how bad might the people in prison be? I really didn't want to think about it, and I knew better than to say anything about that to the rest of the guys. If we were enjoying the fruits of the high-budget dollars and supplies being sent our way, there was a good reason for it. Insurgent activity was way up. It seemed like Iraq was in the middle of an all-out civil war, with us caught in the middle.

On the plus side, we were going out in a small group. Two Stryker drivers, my buddy Richie, our tank commander, me, and two sets of nine-man assault teams, along with RWS operators. One thing that was different about this operation was that it was going to go on during broad daylight—something that up to that point I hadn't experienced.

So, there I was in love and hate and impatient mode. Not too happy about having to resume my duties as a Stryker driver, not too happy about having to head back home because I was just finally starting to get into the rhythm of Iraq and it being my home, hoping for an opportunity to do something different while out, but definitely on edge about these bad guys and how they'd managed to take control of that detention center.

Route Tampa was like a boring stretch of nearly arrow-straight interstate highway back home. As soon as we got out of the compound, I hit the throttles and had the thing doing its top speed—about sixty miles an hour. Operating in daylight was a revelation. The viewing screen was pretty clear, the road not curvy, and the traffic not heavy. The bad part about being out at daylight was that my internal clock was all messed up. For most of those ninety days we'd worked the overnight shift. Even though the sun was climbing in the sky, my body was telling me that I should be hunkering down in my bed and racking out. Feeling sleepy and super-heated, I was soon drowsy. We rattled and bounced along for an hour. Over the comms I joined the rest of the guys talking about how much they did not want to be out there that day.

"This is going to suck," I said.

"Take it easy there, driver," Gonzales said. "We're the ones going for a stroll in Iraq."

"Yeah, driver. Make sure you get us some groceries

while we're out. You got the list I gave you?" added another voice I couldn't quite identify. All their laughter blended into a chorus of kidding.

I switched on my ear protection to quiet the guys and the engine noise. I nearly threw the damn things down when a loud, piercing wail of a sound punched my eardrums. Even at that point, my hearing loss was mounting, thanks to the sound of the weapons and those devices that sometimes seemed like they did more harm than good.

I'd been lazy and didn't want to make the pain of being overheated any greater than it had to be; I'd opted not to wear my hard-plate armor, just the soft plate. I figured I was just going to be like a mom doing the run to soccer practice. Dropping the kids off while they did their thing. Pretty soon the guys' voices went mute, and I figured they were nodding off back there. Too bad there wasn't a drive-thru window I could stop at to get a shot of caffeine.

I was startled by the metallic sound of something rattling around in the cabin.

"Grenade!"

"Frag!"

"Frag!"

We were nearing an overpass, and my mind was already on the fact that a while back one of our Strykers, driving along with the hatch open, had had a grenade dropped into it from the roadway above.

My heart skipped a bunch of beats and I felt like my bowels had emptied. Then I figured out what was going on.

"Dudes—not funny, man." I said over the comms.

I heard their collective laughter again.

They'd done this a few times before, taking a fired .50-cal brass casing and tossing it around. It produced a sound almost exactly like that of a grenade's firing pin being dropped inside what I thought of as our steel casket.

The shot of adrenaline that coursed through me woke me up for a bit, but inevitably it faded and I was once again struggling to stay awake. The sun was angling down at my four o'clock, and I could see drivers going in the opposite direction holding an arm up to keep their vision clear.

As we neared the objective, we got off of Route Tampa, taking a few chewed-up secondary roads, goat paths essentially, and eventually left any kind of roadway at all. We rolled over the desert terrain, slowing then to about twenty miles an hour. At least the rattling and the jostling kept me from falling asleep. We stopped a little less than a quarter mile from a large multistory building standing in mostly level desert. A few dunes dotted the landscape, along with a few palm trees.

I came to a halt and heard the hydraulics kick in as the rear door lowered. A moment later, the assault team fanned out. I opened the hatch and climbed up to get a better view of what was going on, exposing my head and chest to the hot air and a slight breeze. The Iraqi guards came charging toward us. At least I hoped that they were the guards. I'd heard about a number of instances when the bad guys had disguised themselves as members of the Iraqi security forces or police forces and torn up the good guys.

"What a freakin' mess," Richie said. "Those d-bags better get down or they're going to get lit up."

I heard our guys yelling that order, but it didn't seem to be sinking in. Eventually, through an interpreter, our assault team was able to get a better idea of what the situation was. We were going to have to clear the prison, cell by cell, and also try to track the few escapees. Our guys were doing interrogations on the fly, rounding up a few more of the prisoners who'd wandered out of the building, and, based on the sound of the flash bangs coming from inside the detention center, beginning the clearing operation.

With things in good shape, Richie and I took it easy. Our RSW gunner, James, was manning his station and doing all the overwatch we felt was needed.

Along with being tired and a bit dehydrated, I was hurting for some nicotine. I reached into a pocket and pulled out a pack of potent Iraqi cigarettes. They were tiny in comparison to the Marlboro Reds I usually smoked, but packed such a punch that we all referred to them as Red Rockets. The first time I smoked one, I got so light-headed and queasy I thought I was going to puke.

Richie looked at me and shook his head. "How can you do that to yourself?"

I shrugged. "I need something to clear my head."

He took off his sunglasses and rubbed his eyes and squinted, surveying the scene.

"Well, before you get too high and get out of your brain, get us on top of this hill. Better vantage point."

I liked Richie and he had graduated from Ranger School and I hadn't yet, but I mentally questioned this move. Going up there would silhouette us. Placing that big vehicle up on a high point, with nothing for us to blend into, would make us an easier target. To that point, I had no reason to believe that we were dealing with anyone other than those prisoners. Still, I did as Richie asked.

The hill wasn't all that high, maybe fifty feet tall, but the climb up was steep. The Stryker groaned a bit and the engine lugged some as we rose at about a 40-degree angle to the top of that berm. Whatever thoughts I had about us being in an exposed position disappeared for a few moments when I took in the view from up there. It seemed as if all of Iraq was spread out below us. With the sun lowering in the sky, everything was bathed in a yellow-gold haze. Wispy funnels of smoke rose up from trash and cooking fires, looking like a kid's chalk scrawls.

I pulled out my M4, with its little Advanced Combat Optical Gunsight (ACOG) scope, and began to survey the area. I watched as villagers went from house to house carrying pots and cups of tea. The wind kicked up a bit and carried the smell of fried bread. My stomach grumbled, and I tried to think of how many hours had passed since I ate.

"Irv, don't shoot anybody today," Richie said with enough of a note of irritation in his voice to let me know that he was both kidding and serious.

"I'm not, man. Just looking around."

"Well, sometimes I think you confuse the word 'looking' with 'shooting,'" he said. "Like maybe you've got some special form of dyslexia."

I grunted a laugh. That was a new version of a familiar joke. As a newer guy, I sometimes took advantage of my lower rank and status to shoot now and let my superiors do the explaining and the paperwork later. If I saw a guy with a weapon, I wouldn't call it up to get the okay. That left my team leader in a bad spot sometimes.

"Get down! Get down!" Richie's voice cut through my grogginess.

I ducked back inside the hatch. Overhead I heard what reminded me of the rustling sound of papers being fanned or a deck of cards being bridged.

What the heck was that?

A few seconds later, I got the answer. No more than a few yards behind us a mortar round impacted with a somewhat muffled roar and a belch of smoke and sand.

Holy shit! We're being bombed!

More mortar rounds came in, and at that point my training took over. Over the comms I heard us being ordered to get out of there. I was already in the process of doing that. I had the engines fired up. I engaged the drive, heard the motor rev up—but we didn't move. I repeated the process of engaging the drive. Still nothing.

Shrapnel thunked off the thick armor plate, a dull sound that didn't echo at all. I thought we were in pretty good shape, but I worried that a mortar would come in high above us and drop down. We had no armor plate on that top deck; we would have been in bad shape if that happened. Plus, Richie was up there. He was firing at random with his M4, but I knew that those rounds wouldn't reach anyone or anything; we were too far from any position from where the mortars might be firing. I'd been scoping the area and had seen nothing that was within the effective firing range of that weapon.

One of the assault teams came streaming out of the building to assist us. At the same time I heard Cobra attack helicopters flying above us, joined by the sound of their rockets being fired at a position about a half-mile downrange from our location. Based on their impact points, I could now see that in a shallow ravine a shit trench bisected the open ground outside the village. The Cobra pilot was coming in, firing off four or five rockets, overflying, and then returning to do the same. I wasn't sure if Richie could tell what direction the rocket fire was being directed at.

"Right there! Right there! Eight o'clock!"

With my ACOG, I could then see a few dark shapes moving along the lighter color of the sand. The RSW's .50-caliber rounds were kicking up dust as they impacted near that ravine. I could see the bad guys skirmishing along the trench. Our rockets and other rounds seemed to be having no effect on them. They had pretty good cover, and the rocket's blast moved up and out. So with those Hajis down low in that embankment, things were looking pretty good for them.

All this time, I was trying to get the Stryker moving. The assault team was now taking pretty heavy fire; they needed me to close the gap between our positions. I kept jamming on that lever, but finally, I let it sit for a second or two and then eased it in. Finally, the Stryker lurched a bit and then, being in the lowest gear, took off like a jackrabbit. I still had the hatch open, and overhead mortars traced arcs in the sky. The assault team had pressed themselves into the sand to return fire, four or five hundred yards from the berm we were now descending. I was worried about stabbing the front end of the thing into the more level area, but we managed it.

All of what I was seeing was so vivid compared to witnessing operations through night vision. I could actually see human figures; they weren't just black blobs.

Also, from the back of my mind another thought came charging forward—we were seriously outnumbered. There were only twenty-four of us total, a lot less than our usual forty or so. We had mortars coming down on us and AK rounds slicing through the air.

Once I'd closed the gap on our assaulters, I popped up out of the hatch with my M4 and began returning fire. For a long time, I'd thought of myself as Robin to the assault team's Batman. At that moment, though, I wasn't the Boy Wonder—I was doing what all the rest of the guys had been. I thought about all those times when I'd taken out a bad guy and forced others to make things right on my behalf. I didn't like that feeling at all. I should have been more responsible and thought about the consequences of what I was doing. I was so anxious to fit in and do what the rest of the guys were doing that I lost my patience and discipline. Weird thing was, as I was hanging out of the hatch and firing, contributing in a way that I should have been, I really didn't have to exercise any kind of firing discipline at all. Strange how that was working out.

Even though things were pretty hectic, I was engaged in two things at the same time—laying down fire and also thinking about what that all meant. I could hear, for the first time really, what the sound of my M4 firing was really all about. The M4 was unsuppressed and it boomed and vibrated the air around me, and I thought that the sound alone could have killed somebody.

With my mag empty, I took the time to reload and rethink. I had been experiencing a kind of firing frenzy. All those rounds I'd spent were useless. I wasn't really doing what I'd been trained to do, using the skills that I'd refined. I was, in some ways, no better than the undisciplined Iraqis, with their spray and pray. I told myself to calm down, actually put some rounds on target.

As much as I had more visual clarity in the daytime than I ever had experienced before, the sounds of all those different kinds of rounds going off sharpened into a kind of symphony. I played music as a kid and liked orchestral stuff, and just like if you listened close enough to a piece of music you could hear the different instruments contributing to the overall sound, that was what I started to hear: Above the tympani of the M4 and AK rounds, I could hear something that didn't fit in. The .50-cal rounds sounded like something only a synthesizer could produce, something electric, what I imagined as the high-pitched sound a laser might make if it was audible, something menacing. I could also see those large rounds moving through the air and had no doubt about the kind of havoc they could wreak on a human body.

As much as a .50-cal round could do damage to your body, so could all the sights and sounds in a firefight affect your mental, emotional, and physical states. Even though I'd told myself that I needed to calm down, I really hadn't. You hear all of those other rounds being fired, guys yelling and screaming, helicopters buzzing around, and you get caught up in all of that excitement, you find yourself trying to keep up with that crazed tempo.

I shut my eyes to decrease the amount of stimulation I was taking in, borrowing one of the techniques that Carlos Hathcock used to help calm himself. I took a few deep breaths and tried to get inside my own bubble, be free of all the distractions that surrounded me. I opened my eyes again, aimed, and fired. We call that a clean shot. You let it go and it's kind of refreshing, like a deep exhale coming out of your weapon. All the other ones that I'd been firing had been these dirty, exasperated, impatient shots. They had no real purpose or intent. They were like the senseless barking and snapping and growling that one dog engages in because another dog is barking and acting out.

Later on, when I was back home and people would ask me about our operations and I'd tell them that in the helicopter flights we'd often fall asleep, they couldn't understand how we'd done that. But we had to, in a way. That was a way to get us clean.

After I took that brief time-out, I assessed the situation. I realized that by coming down off that berm, we'd actually closed the distance between the bad guys in the trench and ourselves. We were in effective firing range, but I'd been still firing as if those shots were only serving as a distraction to the bad guys. I then understood that I could actually do some damage, be more effective than simply adding to the chaos and confusion.

I continued to focus on my breathing. Through my ACOG, I picked out one of the Hajis. He must have been either one of the tallest of the bunch or one the dumbest, because he was more exposed than any of the others. His head was fully exposed. I could make out the ruddy color of his skin, the uneven growth of his beard, full along his chin and sparse near his cheekbones. I gauged the wind and aimed just to his right. I released all the tension in my body and sent the round. A moment later, I saw the guy's head flop back, his hair whipping like a crazed rocker riffing on his guitar. He didn't come back up.

We'd been on-site for a little less than an hour at that point. The Cobra had run out of rockets and was now popping flares down on their position. Fewer mortar rounds flew overhead. The war song was winding down to a brief coda. I'd fired a few more rounds, but we were going to pull out of there. The guys moved toward the back of the Stryker to load up. They were so drenched in sweat that it dripped off their armor. Even among all the smells of the diesel fuel, hydraulic fluid, and the weapons we'd discharged, their body odor carried to my position. I slammed the hatch shut and with a few final tinks off our armor plate, we were headed back to Route Tampa. I eased the Stryker into top gear and waited for it to speed up.

Behind me, I heard the guys yelling at me, "Get this thing moving!"

I hadn't been thinking. I thought that top gear meant top speed. The engine was lugging, trying to match its revs to the cogs in the transmission. We were puttering along because I'd been rushing things again. I dropped it down into third and at that point vehicle speed, engine speed, and gearing all meshed and worked together. By the time we got back on the main route, we were booking it.

A half hour later, the adrenaline buzz had worn off and my eyes were closing and my head was bobbing.

"Irv, you okay?" Richie's voice startled me.

"I'm good."

"Then keep this thing tracking straight. You're swerving all over."

I did something then that I frequently did on those long drives when I was getting bleary-eyed and nearly delirious. I asked God to send someone out to shoot at us. I didn't need a full-on firefight or an ambush, and definitely not an IED, just something to give me a bit of a rush, something to get the adrenaline flowing. I waited and waited, and eventually my patience was rewarded. A few rounds bounced harmlessly off our armor.

"Ambush! Ambush! Ambush!" I heard Cole, the RWS gunner on the other Stryker, report. We were moving past a roadside market, a few low-slung buildings alongside the road. We were moving at top speed and I knew that unless the bad guys were in a technical paralleling us, we were in no real danger. Still, that was enough to get the juices flowing. I thought of the guy earlier in the day giving me crap about buying the groceries while they went to work.

Well, I'd done more than just been their car service for the day. At that point, I knew that I needed to keep my focus on my job. While Richie fired over the heads of the people at the market, I saw a few guys firing on us, but they'd drop the weapons and immerse themselves in the crowd. I hated that. Why couldn't they just hang in there, give us time to shoot back?

One guy did, and he paid the price for it. I saw him get struck in the chest by a .50-caliber round. The sight was almost cartoonish. It was like the round disintegrated his torso, but his shirt stayed intact. It hung there for a moment while his legs continued to move forward for a few more paces before they collapsed to the ground.

We got back to our compound without another incident. We had just an hour or so to shower up and then get on the bus to get to our flight out of Iraq. I was in no hurry to go home. Even though I'd shot that one guy, I thought more about all the ways in which I'd messed up that day. Part of it was because I'd gotten complacent and accepted too easily my role as Robin. Another reason was that I'd allowed myself to get caught up in the frenzy of the firefight. Striking a balance between assertive and patient was something that I was definitely going to have to work on. I wanted to be back out there, to prove to myself, more than to the others, that I had what it took to be a good soldier. I was going to have to wait and see what the future held for me—what schools I might be assigned to, what other kind of training we'd be engaged in.

Somewhere over Europe, I sat in the plane, the rest of the guys all dozing off in their Ambien sleep, the breathing nearly synchronized, wishing that I could be enjoying that kind of rest. My mind was a jumble of desires and regrets, unsure of whether to focus on what was ahead or what was behind me. I shut my eyes and at some point, the darkness overtook me.

FOUR

SOMEONE TO WATCH OVER US

"WITHOUT WARNING; WITHOUT REMORSE."

That's the motto that snipers live by. I was fortunate that my early interest in becoming a sniper turned out to be my reality. I transformed myself, with the help of a lot of instructors, a lot of patience and persistence, into the guy who became known as The Reaper. Before that, though, as I made the transition to a Sniper Team Leader, I learned over time another important lesson: to trust my gut instincts.

That's not easy to do, especially when you're in the environment that existed in Iraq as the war wound down. The same was true in Afghanistan. At the time I was a Stryker driver/machine gunner, I don't think I appreciated fully how simple my life was. I'd go out and do my job and go back to base and get ready to do it all over again. I didn't have to file any after action reports. That was up to my team leaders, guys like Juan and Richie. I knew that we were responsible collectively for keeping track of the number of killed in action (KIA) that we accumulated on our operations. Every time any of us, whether we were an assaulter, a mortar guy, or a grunt on the ground, believed we had evidence to support a claim that we'd killed a bad guy, we'd call it up to our platoon sergeant or ground force commander to have that kill noted. We weren't into keeping track of our individual accomplishments, but it seemed like those in charge of us, because of what was being handed down to them from Washington, were really concerned about accounting and accountability.

The rules of engagement dictated much of our lives outside the wire, and as I rose through the ranks, I saw how they also figured in what we did once back inside the wire after an operation and engaging with the enemy. One of the first tasks that I had to get used to was doing a body count and inspection after an engagement. A couple of guys in the unit were issued digital cameras and were tasked with taking photos of the KIA to demonstrate that it was a "good" kill, meaning they'd been armed. We'd walk among the dead guys taking photos of the bodies, their weapons, spent shells, anything at all to prove that we'd followed the ROEs. Doing all this was such an established part of the routine that I didn't really think much about the why of it all. I knew that it made me feel good to see the dead guys there. That was proof that we were doing our jobs and taking down people who wanted to destroy America and our way of life any way they possibly could.

I don't think that I would like a job where at the end of the day I didn't have some evidence of what I'd accomplished. It's kind of like if you worked construction and walked to your truck at quitting time and looked back and saw that the second story of the house had been framed that day and the job site looked different as a result. You could point to it and say, "We did that," and it would be obvious to anyone paying attention that the building looked different, no doubt about it.

Taking the time to photograph those bodies seemed worth it, even though it exposed us to more risk; most of the time I was on the perimeter facing out to provide security for the guys doing the actual photography and searching for documents and other forms of intel. It gave me some validation, which was important. I didn't think a whole lot about what it meant in terms of policy and perception. That would come later, after I'd become a sniper and had a couple of my kills called into question by investigators from outside my direct chain of command. That happened to me twice, when I experienced something that was something like what a person unjustly accused of a crime might go through. You know what you did, but when you get asked all kinds of questions and have things turned around and kind of twisted, you start to doubt yourself. You start to question, not so much what you saw and what you did, but whether or not it was worth feeling this way about yourself.

I go back to our sniper's motto: "Without warning; without remorse." I can't say that I felt remorse for taking out the bad guys that I did. It's way more complicated than feeling good or feeling bad. Some of it had to do with the feeling that maybe there were some people—people outside the units I served with—who had doubts about my integrity. That's a tough thing to swallow, having your judgment and your intentions called into question. I was out there, the rest of us were out there, putting our lives on the line. But either back home or in other commands, people were to either a small or a large degree questioning what I was doing. Hard to shut all of that out, but in the heat of the moment, when the battle's raging, the last thing you want to do is worry about that stuff.

In the potentially disastrous friendly-fire instances I wrote about earlier, I'm damn glad that I did hesitate and I did worry about reviews. I was the new guy and didn't have much experience to rely on. As I spent more time downrange and as I talked with guys who'd seen a lot more action than I did and learned from them, I started to trust myself a whole lot more. Funny thing is, as I write this now, I only realize fully just how much "oversight" there was on our actions. With the drones and other aircraft flying above us, there was an eye in the sky looking down on us at all times. There were a few times when I was a part of that eye-in-the-sky group and, to be honest, I liked having my boots on the ground a whole lot better.

In case you haven't read my first book, let me make one thing clear: I don't like heights. I'm okay flying in the helicopters, but just as a means to get someplace quickly so that I can get back on the ground and do my job. I admire the pilots and crews that fly those things, but I would never want to be one of them. So with that in mind, you can probably understand why I was a bit apprehensive when, in late spring of 2009, my spotter Mike Pemberton and I got the call, along with eight other guys, to report to the TC for a briefing. Mike and I took our seats and looked at the roster and saw something odd.

"What's up with this?" I asked Mike.

"Damned if I know," he said, running his finger down the list.

Our names weren't there. Normally, anytime anybody went out on an operation, the sniper teams went along in support of them.

As the briefing went on, we learned that we'd be going along on the operation as what I guess you could call aerial "squirter" stoppers. "Squirters" were any of the enemy who tried to flee the position where our operation was taking place. Normally, Mike and I would be positioned somewhere on the ground, generally at a high vantage point, so that we could spot them and shoot them.

Not this time.

Instead, we were going to fly around in a second Chinook helicopter while the rest of the team went in on another and performed the operation. If anyone tried to flee the objective, we'd fire from the belly of the bird at them. Now, some guys really got off on doing that kind of flying and firing, but not me. Nor was it just my fear of heights that had me anxious on these kinds of operations—and this was my first one ever downrange. Firing from a moving aircraft, even one that was hovering, required a different mind-set and technique than firing from the ground. At Sniper School and later, between deployments, we trained to do this, but I didn't like it at all. I was a perfectionist, and my accuracy suffered when I was up there firing at targets. I've even taken part in shooting competitions from helicopters, and I never score nearly as high in those than I do in any of the others.

Now, it was different when we didn't fire from above but landed the bird ahead of the squirters, dismounted, and fired from a fixed position. I didn't like all the up and down and rapid ascents and descents, but at least I was firmly connected to Mother Earth when I had the weapon in my hands. Unless you've done it, it's hard to imagine how much vibration and bouncing around goes on when you're in a helicopter with its turbine engines going. Just trying to keep the weapon steady for a second to look through the scope sometimes takes monumental effort. But like I said, it was a different deal when the choppers just got us from point to point a lot more quickly than we could have gone on foot or in a ground vehicle.

Mike and I got pretty good at that, especially since from up above it was easy to spot a good hide from which we could set up our sniper position. I liked the improvisational nature of those operations as well. We'd get to one area, do our thing, see some other activity, head over there, and on and on, stringing them together without having to do a brief or debrief in between. It was like running a fast-break offense in basketball or the kind of high-tempo stuff without a huddle that a lot of football teams now use, run and gun and all that.

So there Mike and I were in the belly of a Chinook along with a bunch of other guys while our regular assault team was in another bird about to be set down below us somewhere in Helmand Province. While a bunch of the other soldiers tried to grab a quick nap, I sat listening to the radio as our assaulters went in. Before we lost radio feed, it seemed as if everything was going to plan.

"Everything's cool," I told Mike. "We can just chill."

"I'm good to go with that," he said.

I sat there staring into the middle distance, not a whole lot on my mind other than how numb my butt was starting to feel. I was also thinking about Jessica, a woman I'd just started to exchange communications with back home via Myspace. I also wondered what some of my buddies back home were up to, if they were studying for a test or just hanging out drinking and playing video games.

Then, without anything happening that I could detect, the rest of the guys on board all started stirring around. I crawled over to the assault team squad leader so that I could be heard above the engine's roar.

"What's going on?"

Jackson, an African-American from Fort Lauderdale who used to crack me up with his ability to sing really high and hit notes like Mariah Carey, said, "We're about to land. Your guys need some backup."

Jackson shrugged and patted his pockets before taking out a stick of gum and unwrapping it.

I figured either the guys had gotten into a firefight or the squirters needed tracking. I went back to my seat and pointed to the floor of the helicopter, indicating to Mike that we were going in. I couldn't respond to Mike's question about what was happening. All I knew was they were descending crazy fast. Mike was on one knee, and I got down beside him in the same position.

We bumped fists and wished each other good luck like we usually did. As the chopper's skids hit the turf and dust rose up, I yelled at Mike, "Let's do this thing."

Instead of being at the front like we normally were, Mike and I were the last ones off the bird. I watched us scatter to our positions and it was weird but cool to be able to account for every one of us. With just ten of us now on the ground, I felt like I was a Delta Force guy doing some real high-speed gig. I couldn't help but smile at the thought of that. This was my first time with such a small group, and I liked the flexibility of it all. Who knew what we might be called on to do? Sure, we all had our assignments, but when you're out there with such a small group, the chances of having to take on some other task were greater. I also felt a greater sense of responsibility toward the other members of this small element. You always relied on other people, but this was different just because the numbers were so low.

I surveyed the surroundings and, instead of the usual low-scrub, high-altitude desert I was so accustomed to seeing, in front of me spread a clump of tall trees covering about the area of a city block. A small section had been cleared in the center of that wooded area and in that space a neat rectangular house sat. The scene was almost pretty, and I could imagine what it might have been like to be out there in that solitude and with those trees to give you even more privacy and a break from the relentless wind. I'd heard guys use the term "God's Country" when talking about places that they wanted to settle someday back in the States; I wondered briefly if it was terrain like this that they had in mind.

I didn't have too long to think about it. I looked at the GPS unit and listened through our air link to the intel we were getting. Four to six squirters. RPGs. AK47s. Most likely to the north of our location, beyond the house and the clearing surrounding it. That meant in the tree line beyond. Not good. Lots of places for them to hide and a good vantage point for them to shoot and pick us off. Within a few seconds, a plan was formulating. As we ran the three hundred or so yards through that clearing, I kept thinking, "This could be bad. Really bad."

A few seconds after we ran by the house, we heard over the comms, "You passed it. You passed it. You overran the objective."

We were still running. I looked over at the squad leader and I could see the confusion in his expression. He raised his hand and we all came to a stop. I eased up my night vision to get a better sense of where we were and the lay of the land. A perfectly sliced half moon was in the sky and everything was washed in a grayish light. The house sat there, dark and silent.

Why hadn't they opened up on us as we ran past? Did they think we'd just keep right on going and then they'd slip out behind us and head back in the other direction?

I considered the options. I had my SR-25 long rifle with me and I could, if necessary, join the guys in clearing that house. It wouldn't be ideal, but I could. Mike had his bolt-action, and that wasn't going to be of much use; the best he could have done was taken up the tail position among the assaulters. We were only ten guys total and, given the number of Hajis we were told might be in there, we didn't have overwhelming numbers. Maybe we were going to be needed.

The team leader gets everybody grouped up and then they take a position along an outside wall of the house, stacked up against one another. He wanted us to do our usual thing, so Mike and I took positions about fifty yards from the house—me at a position where I could see the front entry of the building, Mike at the rear. The team was in my line of sight and once the second man gave the first a quick squeeze on the shoulder, they busted inside. I heard the muffled sound of a few flash bangs going on, but nothing else until the all clear came over the comms just a few seconds later.

What the hell?

Turned out nobody was inside. But there were a whole lot of *things* inside. The guys started carrying out bags and bags of refined heroin, unrefined opium, and pods of poppy. We also suspected that some of the other bags they found contained bomb-making materials. None of us were experts on what they looked or smelled like and we didn't have a working dog with us to help us out, so the assault team guys just added it to the pile they were building in front of the porchlike entryway at the front of the house.

Mike and I had taken position to do overwatch, each of us taking half of the 180-degree view in front of us. I knew what was going on, but the wind freshened, and the smell of plastic bags being burned, along with their contents, had my eyes stinging a bit. Smoke from the fire swirled around me and I stepped a few paces further

downrange to be away from it. Whatever I'd been thinking before about this setting being a part of God's Country was gone. I was glad that we'd made that find and
discovered this cache. It was good to know that not only
would we be hitting the Taliban's ability to finance operations, but that those drugs weren't going to end up on the
streets of Miami or somewhere else in the world.

Half-joking and half-serious because I had no idea
how heroin got abused, I said to the assault team leader,
"We better get the hell out of here before we all get
messed up by that heroin smoke."

He shook his head. "No worries about that, Irv. That
won't hurt us, but we're out of here in a few anyway."

We were waiting for more intel to come in about those
squirters—they had to have gone somewhere. I scanned
the area in front of me and wondered if they were somewhere just outside our vision, pissed as all hell that we'd
burned up their stuff and just waiting for the right moment to attack.

Once the fire had died down a bit, we moved to another position, dropping down into a dry riverbed eight
hundred or so yards from the house. A few large rocks
sat scattered among the loose stones beneath our feet.
Beyond the riverbed to the west was an open area the
length of a football field and more trees. A couple of
houses sat on the perimeter of that stand of trees; it was
massive by Afghan countryside standards—three floors
and, alongside it, a slightly smaller home. A small wooden

bridge, spanning another dry irrigation ditch, stood sentry, allowing access to the houses.

I can't really explain why, but I was suddenly struck by a sense that something wasn't right. This was different than me being on high alert and wondering about those squirters. Something just didn't seem right about this whole situation.

"Mike, you have that feeling?"

"I sure do. I don't like this at all."

I could feel the hairs standing up on the back of my neck. Suddenly, I was back at home as a kid going up the darkened stairs to my room feeling like some monster loomed behind me.

"I got the same thing, Irv. I got the same thing." Something about Pemberton talking again and repeating himself intensified the feeling. Plus, by this time I'd been in country over the course of 5th deployment, 700 plus days, and 552 operations, and I'd learned to trust my gut.

I looked at my watch. The copters were about five minutes out.

"We should hunker down a bit," I said.

Mike and I dropped a bit lower into the riverbed, still keeping our eyes high enough to see over the bank into the tree line.

As soon as I'd settled in and moved a few rocks out of the way so that I could rest my elbows more comfortably on the ground, I saw tracers and heard their *snap, snap, snap,* just overhead.

It freaked me out a bit to think of what had been going on for the last hour or so. We'd come after these guys. They weren't where we'd been told they were. Now, after we'd moved along into a new position for an extraction, they decided to try to ambush us. We could see that the tracers were coming from multiple locations within those two buildings and from a few holed up in the tree line.

We spread out and the machine gunners and the lightweight gunners laid down some suppressive fire. We were only a hundred yards from those houses, close enough that I could see the tracers leaving the muzzles of the enemy's weapons and follow them.

"Holy shit," I thought, "this is scary."

Their rounds were coming low to the ground, and I hated that. I wanted to run to get into a more protected position, but with them low-firing, the thought of getting kneecapped stopped me. Pemberton and I weren't in the best position relative to the house, either. We were on the extreme far left of the rest of the unit, closer to the building than anyone else. Worse, a few trees stood between us and the house. It gave us some protection, but not as clear of a line of sight as I would have liked.

The rest of the team was focusing their fire on the tree line, but I knew that if I was one of those Hajis, I'd have wanted to be in one of those upper windows of the two houses. So that's where I focused my attention. Sure enough, one of the bad guys popped up in the window,

sprayed a few rounds, and then ducked back for cover.
Every few seconds, he'd do the same thing. I just waited
and watched and counted.

He'd pop and shoot. A thousand one. A thousand
two. A thousand three. Pop and shoot. A thousand one.
A thousand two. A thousand three.

I knew I had him. I focused on the corner of the
window he would appear in, and after he disappeared I
counted to two and fired even before I saw him. Easy
pickings. He went down. From a hundred yards that
was no big deal, but I owed credit to my idol, Carlos
Hathcock, the greatest sniper of the Vietnam War, or
any war as far as I was concerned. I read his book as a
kid and watched a documentary about him. In this situation, I relied on something the bad guy did that Carlos Hathcock had said was one of the deadliest sins you
could commit as an active shooter. That bad guy in the
window had fallen into a rhythm and a pattern that I
could easily figure out. Once I understood the timing
and got the tempo, the rest was just the most basic marks-
manship that any soldier has mastered.

Just to be sure I'd gotten the guy, I pointed my spotlight into that window and ran it all around the window
frame. The edges of it were splotched with dark. The same
was true of the wall beyond the window. That wasn't
messy housekeeping; that was the dude's recently spattered blood. All of that—from me spotting him to figuring out his pattern to spotlighting the area—took less

than fifteen seconds. But it seemed like time had really slowed, as it often did during those firefights. It's weird, and it's nearly impossible to describe that sensation of time slowing like that. People moved at a normal rate, but it was as if everything else around them was frozen.

I looked at Mike, and he was scanning the tree line and then over to the house and then to our flank on the far right, making sure no one breached our line.

From within the tree line, I saw four distinct muzzle flashes. I wasn't so concerned about the number, but about how those flashes were arrayed. These guys knew what they were doing! One flash out front, another a few yards behind the first, and then the same thing for the other two. With that kind of depth it was going to be hard to get a good gauge on their distance and location.

Then, for some reason, their fire ceased completely. I looked over at Mike. He was still scanning. I grabbed at his ankle.

"Move. Move. Move. There. Now."

I don't why it was, but I always had a hard time talking in complete sentences in the middle of a firefight. I was scared and that had a lot to do with it, but it was like my mouth couldn't keep up with what my mind was telling me. Fortunately, Mike and I had been together for a while, and he and I had developed an instinctual understanding of some kind.

In my mind, I was hearing myself say this: "Mike.

Hey, man, let's get up and push way far left, because I think these guys are going to try to flank us. So we better hustle over to the tree line over there and make sure no one gets past us. Got it? Okay. Let's go."

Mike got my much shorter message. We took off running with me in the lead, both of us bent at the waist trying to make ourselves as small as possible while still making good time. I always wanted to be out in front of him, even if that meant that I was in line to take a shot instead of him. I was the squad leader and that meant being out in front. Bullets were striking and skipping between the two of us and I kept thinking, "Oh shit, oh shit, oh shit," in time with my footsteps. That was a variation on what we'd learned in training—"I'm up, you see me, I'm down. I'm up. You see me. I'm down."

We took our far-left position and then I radioed the squad leader to let him know where we were. We figured we were going to settle in there for as long as this was going to take. We both were scanning the tree line, Mike through his scope, me with just my naked eye. Behind one of the skinniest trees, I thought I detected some motion.

"See that?" I asked.

"Roger that, Irv."

We confirmed our suspicion: These dudes were trying to flank us. The right thing to do, probably, but one of the Hajis picked the wrong tree to use as a backrest. The tree was maybe six to ten inches in circumference and parts of his back spread out well beyond its edges. I could see other trees just a few feet from that one that were much wider. Why he settled on that one, I have no idea.

"You seeing this?" Mike hissed, his voice a mix of disbelief and a tiny laugh.

"I am," I said. Then I added, "You got one. You got one," signaling to Mike that I saw that the enemy was armed, which meant we were good to go to shoot him.

Pemberton racked a round.

"Hey, distance?" he asked.

I thought it didn't matter. Anything between a hundred and five hundred yards, Mike could basically hold anywhere on the torso of the target and he'd smack it. With his weapon, one that fired a big flat-flying round, he didn't have to worry too much about the trajectory.

"Dial for two," I told him, indicating that he didn't really have to make much of an adjustment, just hold under the target slightly.

Mike let one rip and watched as the trunk of that skinny little tree sparked. The guy behind it twitched a bit, but didn't go down.

That was a good shot even if he didn't hit the guy. As direct-action snipers, our tactics and aim weren't as precise as long-range guys. We didn't have the time in that situation to sit there and fully set up with a tripod and do all kinds of calculations and fine-tune our aim and use laser rangefinders and other bits of technology. Mike knew not to go for a head shot; heads move too much. He went for a center mass shot.

"Hit him. Hit him. Hit him," I said. Mike didn't need me to tell him what to do, but I was so pumped I couldn't keep my mouth shut.

Mike must have adjusted his aim a bit because the next round he fired didn't hit the tree at all. I heard the round striking flesh with a *smack-pop*, and the guy was down.

I scanned away from that skinny tree and thought I saw one or two more targets in that same small area. I was absolutely certain of one of them. He was using a partially fallen tree to brace his AK as he sprayed fire toward our assault team's position. When I say "toward," I really mean *toward* it and not *at* it. Our guys were firing at him and I saw tree bark and dirt clods flying all around the guy. He had to be scared shitless and was just shutting his eyes and squeezing the trigger. The barrel of the gun was pointed midway between ground and sky. I'd seen that so many times and I'd come to believe, like a lot of our guys did, that those dumbshits believed that God's will was truly what determined who got shot and who didn't. Aim and firing discipline had nothing to do with it. If you were meant to kill a guy, God would make that bullet find its way home.

"Dumbass," I thought. I focused on his muzzle flash and then aimed for that. I was dialed in for the distance and figured that if I was a little high, I'd hit him in the head. If I wasn't high, then I'd likely hit the AK and take that out of commission. I got the guy in the neck and that ended his random AK firing.

During all of this, the squad leader had called in for air assets. I believed there was one or at most two more squirters to be taken out. I couldn't see their exact positions, but it didn't really matter when the bombs started falling out there. By that time, we were in the helicopter and heading out. We were riding high and feeling really good about ourselves.

Back at the joint operations center (JOC), we all gathered around a screen to watch the drone footage. That was one of the best parts of any operation, watching how the day was won.

I didn't mind one bit experiencing that version of someone looking over my shoulder. More than that, though, I was grateful for having more time outside the wire as a sniper developing a kind of sixth sense that was going to help me and the rest of the guys stay safe. Experience was the best teacher out there, and that was something you'd never get from a book or a classroom. As much as all that was in place to help prepare us, I think that more than anything else, it reinforced the idea that no matter what anyone can teach you, you're going to have to learn on your own and be accountable. A lot was at stake, and that helped you develop the skills that you weren't even aware you had and that no simulation could ever bring out in you. Combat shone a light on you and aspects of yourself that would have otherwise never been tested. It was as much a proving ground as a battleground.

FIVE

FINDING YOUR FOCUS ON A HELL NIGHT IN HELMAND

BY THE TIME I LEFT the Army in 2010, I had spent six years with the Special Operations 3rd Ranger Battalion, 75th Ranger Regiment. That meant that I spent thousands and thousands of hours working with many of the same guys over that time. I couldn't know everybody well, obviously, and I had a few guys that I counted as close friends. In lots of ways, being with that group was kind of like going to school with people. We often used the term "grew up in" a regiment to describe the process by which we started out and then, at least in my case, rose through the ranks.

I started out as kind of a runt, not so much in stature but in terms of my rank and my abilities. I was always a good soldier, I'd like to think, but it wasn't until I became a sniper that I really earned the respect of people within the unit. I can't lie and say that it didn't matter what other guys in the battalion thought of me. That's more true of what they thought of me as a soldier than as a person. You're going to bump against some people you work with no matter what, and they may end up not liking you a whole lot. Respect was what I was more concerned about. I could have gone about trying to be a hard-ass, ball-busting, by-the-regulations kind of guy, but that wasn't my personality. I wanted to be respected and I figured one of the best ways to earn that respect was to treat as many people as possible the way that I wanted to be treated. To get respect you've got to give it.

All these years later, I can still feel the pride that welled up inside when we sat in a ready room and listened to a briefing. When Mike or I was mentioned as the sniper going out in support of the other units, I'd catch a few guys nodding appreciatively and some of the younger guys looking over at Mike and me. I could see that they were like I had been back in the day—eager to get some experience and also a little bit hopeful that one day they'd be able to do some of the cool stuff we were doing. I was proud to be the Sniper Team Leader, but I never lorded that over anybody. I liked being trusted to make good decisions and to execute our plan. I was flattered by the attention I got for my individual success, of course, but it was the trust and the responsibility that went along with it that I sometimes miss now that I'm no longer activity duty. It's a little different now that I'm not part of a big team and its success.

We all had each other's backs, but that didn't prevent us from talking behind one another's backs or developing rivalries with other units. Our workplace wasn't that much different from yours. People gossiped about personal stuff they learned about a guy's private life. We also gossiped and speculated about what was going on in a particular unit or team. We were human, and though I write mostly about the action that was taking place on the battlefield, that didn't occupy us 24/7.

I didn't talk a whole lot about my personal life and in particular about my girl back home, Jessica, who is now my wife. Once I called home to talk with Jessica and she brought up the subject of missing a payment on one of our monthly bills. I didn't like the idea of having to pay late fees, but I was fine with it. Not a big deal. What did bug me a bit was that I was calling from Afghanistan. I didn't have a whole lot of time to talk and there were a lot more things on my mind than our utility bills or whatever it was. (I can't remember which one was late, and that just goes to show how unimportant that was to me.)

I didn't want to spend the time talking about it—the reasons why it was late, why she thought the policy was unfair—and it seemed like before we had to break off the conversation, I'd spent more time on something trivial than what I really wanted to talk about. I did something afterward that I seldom did. I talked to Mike and let him know about how the conversation had gone and how down I was about it.

Mike laughed.

So much for an empathetic response.

To be fair, Mike and I didn't know each other that well at the time. Eventually, I got to be pretty close to him, since we worked so closely together and from time to time bunked in the same room. Mike had just come aboard, hadn't gone to Sniper School yet, so it was still early in our relationship.

"Dude, it really bummed me out," I told him.

"That's why I'm single," Mike said, "so I don't have to deal with that kind of thing. I can keep my mind squared away."

"No," I said, "you're single because no one would want to go out with you, let alone marry you."

"Whatever, Irv. I'm not the one whining."

That's what I got for trying to confide in a single guy about a miscommunication with a spouse.

Lesson learned: I decided it was best to keep my grumbling, aka my *whining*, to myself after that. Later on, Mike and I would laugh about that exchange. He'd also get to know Jessica much better and was the guy I trusted to be the one to talk to her if something bad ever happened to me.

The cool thing was that when it was time to go out on an operation, all of that personal stuff just kind of disappeared. Not that we didn't care about one another, but whatever little gossipy things or petty jealousies or whatever didn't influence how we did our jobs. When it was time for us to focus on the task at hand, we were all prepared to set aside everything and do just that. When we got the call, we were all about getting the job done. Off hours, we could mess with one another, pressures and problems from back home could occupy much of our minds, but there was a time and place for that, and you had to develop a mechanism for stowing away distractions.

After February of 2009, when President Obama announced the increase of troops going to Afghanistan, our jobs took on a different dimension from what they'd been in Iraq. Those two roles of peacekeeping and nation building weren't ever really a part of what our 75th Ranger Regiment was called on to do. We were mostly going after high-value targets, and so, in the early spring of 2009, Mike and I were in Helmand Province. We'd come to understand one thing: If President Obama's focus on Afghanistan and winning the Global War on Terrorism had any chance of succeeding, Helmand Province was the place where that was going to be made or broken.

We had a sense that something big was going to be coming our way. We didn't know when, but figured it had to be soon. In the meantime, we had to just keep our focus on the next day, the next operation. It was best not to look at the big picture or to question the larger strategy, but it was human nature to sometimes wonder why certain things were being done.

For example, one afternoon later that spring, we'd done our usual briefing and gone about getting ready to go out on an operation. Word came down that a chaplain was going to be showing up.

"A chaplain?"

"He from Charlie Company?" Laurence asked. He stood there waiting, expecting us to laugh at his little joke. We weren't going to give it to him, especially since it was a lot funnier to see him frown and then begin to squirm. We knew eventually he'd decide to explain the statement, so we left him hanging for a few seconds more. "The guy with the cane and the funny walk. The silent-movie dude?"

"The only silent movie I want to see is of you getting your ass in gear and getting out into the truck," Babcock, one of the assaulters, said.

That got a few hoots and some mock applause.

I was over in a corner with Pemberton as I laced up my boots.

"For real? A chaplain?" I muttered.

"We'll see."

I wasn't much of a praying guy, but I do remember back in high school in the locker room before a football game our coach asking us to bow our heads. I wondered if it was going to be like that. I also wondered if maybe we weren't being told the real deal about this upcoming operation.

I also didn't like having our routine changed. It was almost always: briefing, rest/nap, ready room, truck, fly in. Those routines comforted me and made it easy on me and my mind. After more than a hundred operations, I didn't want to have to do a whole lot of thinking prior to getting out there.

The chaplain came in, and he wasn't a mousy guy like Father Mulcahy I'd seen on reruns of *M*A*S*H* growing up; instead, he was a big beefy lineman type with an incredibly deep voice that could really have been God's. We all gathered around him, and he asked us to bow our heads. I did, and he did about what I'd expected: asked God to watch over all of us. But at the end of all that, he went on and talked about how he wanted God to make sure that our precision rifles, our .308-cals and our .300 Win Mags, would be the instruments to take down our enemies and serve our great purpose. He knew his stuff, and he also made it clear that he believed that we were doing something special and not something that God would look down on us for or punish us for. I never really thought that way, but still, it was good to hear that this chaplain really believed that our cause was just.

It's too bad that he didn't have a pipeline to the gods of technology. After the prayer circle broke up, I put my earpieces in, put the mic up to my mouth, and said, "Mic check. Mic check. Can you read me?"

I waited, and got nothing back.

Not again. This was getting to the point of ridiculousness. The one thing that consistently plagued us was comm failures and problems. That was one form of distraction that none of us needed; the last thing we wanted was for our focus to be compromised, especially in the middle of an operation.

I felt bad for the guys who had to sort those things out for us. They did their best, but the equipment just wasn't reliable. I didn't know much about how the stuff worked, so I had no clue about what was causing all the issues. All I could ever do was just wait in line with the rest of the guys while the technicians tried to sort each of us out. At least we were back on track in terms of our normal routine.

I spoke too soon. One of the bits of gossip that had been going around was that a Tier 1 guy was in our midst. When I left the ready room and went to have a smoke out on the compound, I saw someone who pretty clearly wasn't part of our group waiting among us.

I should take a moment and explain what I mean by "Tier 1." This'll just be a brief overview. The Army Rangers (75th Ranger Regiment), Army Special Forces (Green Berets), and 1st Special Forces Operational Detachment—Delta, the Navy SEALs, and DEVGRU (Naval Special Warfare Development Group, aka SEAL

Team 6)—are all part of the US Special Operations Command (USSOCOM). USSOCOM generally and unofficially divides its various units into a "Tier 1" group and a "Tier 2" group. The Rangers, Green Berets, and "normal" SEALs fall under Tier 2; we're the more conventional SOCOM forces. SEAL Team 6 and Delta guys are considered Tier 1. Tier 1 guys are kind of a combination of a soldier and a spy or an undercover cop. They discard their military uniforms and don't have military-regulation haircuts when they go deep behind enemy lines, usually in teams of no more than three or four.

Some guys in Tier 2 and the regular Army think that the Tier 1 guys are all completely arrogant, but I was willing to give this guy the benefit of the doubt. He had what it took to take on one of the most glamorous, to my mind, roles in the military. He deserved some respect, and I hoped that he'd show some to us. Seeing him walking around and talking to the other guys was a good sign that he wasn't an asshole. Having him along and having the chaplain say those prayers was making me wonder what was really going on here.

Once we were all loaded in for the drive to the airfield, we headed toward the gates.

"Whoa! Whoa! Whoa!" I heard from the back. It was Alvarez. "Got to go back. Tell the driver!"

We relayed the message. At that point, we weren't sure what Alvarez's deal was, so we formed a quick betting pool on what piece of gear he'd forgotten. We watched him trotting back from the ready room with his helmet in his hands.

"Told your dumbass it was his helmet!"

"Aw, man."

I smiled as a chorus of other responses from winners and losers rattled around our minibus.

"Least it wasn't his weapon," Mike said, sliding the words out of the side of his mouth so that only I could hear him.

I had told Mike that I'd done that once in Iraq, and he'd never let me forget it. Worse, I'd gotten on the bus and the first thing I'd said to my buddy Ortiz was, "I feel really lightweight today." Once I eventually figured out why, I was pissed at Ortiz for not telling me. It wasn't really his job, but still I had to take it out on somebody. Hard to believe that you could forget an important piece of gear like a helmet or a weapon, but with the hours we kept and sleepwalking through a lot of the time in the ready room kitting up, at least once every two weeks somebody had to "whoa" the bus.

A couple of times, I didn't realize that I'd forgotten my weapon or some other essential gear until we'd landed and were setting out for the objective. I sometimes felt like I was an obsessive-compulsive disorder sufferer when I'd start patting myself all over doing a quick gear check every few minutes while on the flight out. That night, after we got the one-minute-thirty-second call, Mike and I did the same thing for one another.

Good to go.

As important as it was to have that focus working for you, it often escaped you prior to going out on an operation. Better then, I guess, than in the middle of the action.

The dust had barely settled and our point man had just begun to relay our GPS coordinates when tracer rounds started coming our way. Great. Just another day that the Taliban seemed really determined to put the "hell" in Helmand.

We were still bunched up, with Mike and me doing perimeter duty. I noticed that the Tier 1 guy (who for obvious reasons has to remain identified only to this extent) had come up from the rear. He was just tagging along, but I noticed that he was going over to each of the elements on the operation. He'd say a few words and smile and was just generally seeming like he was there trying to fit in and check in with everybody. I wondered if part of what we were doing that day was helping insert him into a new location.

He came up to Mike and me and said, "Hey, man, you guys ready?"

"We're on this," Mike said.

"Hey, well, watch my back today, okay? Glad to know you guys are out here."

He walked off, and I was feeling pretty good about myself at that point. We all headed out and soon were walking down a narrow alleyway, only wide enough for a moped to fit through. The village was small, maybe a square mile in size with just two or three main arteries running east-west and the same number running north-south. Along those routes a few storefronts stood; there was also a small central area where an outdoor market might be set up. Mike and I were on the far-left edge of the village, and I could see a stand of trees out beyond a pile of rubble and the remains of a low stone wall. Everything around us—the ground, the buildings— were all the same beige-brown color of sand.

Against that backdrop, two shapes, one black and one green, stood out. Two figures in native dress moved through the trees to a house on the edge of the village. Then they retraced their steps and went back into the tree line. I could only catch a partial glimpse of them through the trees—a pair of legs, a torso, then a head bobbing. They did that same back-and-forth thing again.

Our point man stopped. He'd spotted what I'd seen. He was just standing there scanning when he suddenly whipped his head back to the left. He tapped his chest to turn on his comms. I listened in as he reported to the platoon sergeant.

"Two armed targets. I think they're setting up for an ambush."

I didn't have to hear any more. "We're moving."

I was glad that I didn't have to wait for the platoon sergeant to respond and issue an order. That was what was great about a lot of the NCOs: They understood that guys knew what to do and trusted them to make the right moves.

Mike and I made our way ahead of the first and second assault teams to the head of the line. Weapons squad was at our rear.

We were approximately 550 yards from the tree line.

"Let me mil those guys out," I said, looking through my scope. I noticed that a third Haji had joined the other two in doing that walk back and forth. The trio went inside the house. I edged a few steps to get a better view through the trees. I'm glad I did. From that vantage point, I could clearly see an RPK machine gun sitting on a tripod. I scoped around a bit more and saw another box of ammo for the belt-fed weapon sitting on the ground.

"This is Sniper One. Sniper Two and I are about to take these guys out. Stand by."

"Roger that," the platoon sergeant replied. "Make it quiet. Make it quick. We've got to keep moving."

Mike was still learning about his role and how sniping worked, so I asked him, "How far do you think it is to their position?"

I'd already done the computations in my head, doing what I mentioned earlier: "milling it out." The math was relatively simple. I estimated the height of the target's torso—forty inches from his belt line to the top of his head. The distance calculation used a constant of 25.4 to arrive at a value in meters. That meant that

$40 \times 25.4 = 1,016$. Our scopes had markings inside them, and when I refocused on the target, he was twelve dots high. So, I took that number twelve and divided the previous result and came up with 600 to 680 meters, roughly 650 to 750 yards.

Mike came up with the same numbers.

I spread the bipod legs and walked over to a small rise, more of a bump in the ground, and lay down behind my weapon. This was rare for me in my sniper career. Normally, I took a knee instead of lying down, mostly because so many of my shots were from areas where I was in tall grass or had to fire over some other obstacle.

I focused on the first guy.

"I'm going to go in hot," I said. The target was standing behind the machine gun, adjusting some part of it. He was partially bent over but then rose to his full height again. I squeezed the trigger and the guy dropped out of my sight line. While I'd been aiming, I'd tried to visualize what the other two would do so that I could be prepared to move on them and fire again. They did the unexpected.

They froze.

I guessed that this was one of those cases when the expression "didn't know what hit them" was literally true. I was using a suppressor to keep it quiet so they wouldn't know the direction from which the round had come.

A second or two after I fired, Mike let loose a round and took out the second guy.

That left the third guy. He didn't freeze, but it was like he was on a tight leash or something. He'd take a few steps to the right, then to the left, almost like he was a junior high kid awkwardly slow-dancing with an invisible date.

I squeezed off another round and hit him right in the center of his belly. I was feeling pretty good about that for an instant, but the Haji didn't go down. I couldn't believe it. A .308 round from that distance had enough impact velocity on it to knock him clean off his feet. But there he was, still doing that little slow-dance thing. He was bent at the waist at this point, but still shuffling.

What the hell? I was pissed. I was thinking about what the platoon sergeant had said. Quiet and quick. Well, I'd done the quiet thing, but now all of a sudden, this wasn't happening quick. Mike fired again, and he hit the guy. I'd seen through my scope Mike's laser on the target and then a brief glint of light as the bullet passed through my sight and into roughly the same spot on the guy's gut where my round had gone in.

Still, the guy didn't go down.

My mind was racing, not so much about whether we'd encountered the Afghani Superman or something but about the guys in the unit thinking that I'd been missing this target. Then I felt that kick-in-the-balls sensation as I realized that the Tier 1 guy was there witnessing all of this. I didn't talk about it much, but I'd been thinking that it would be cool to try to become a Delta guy. If this was my audition, I was totally screwing it up. I started to rush things, was breathing way too hard, and fired another round that completely missed. I aimed again, now holding my breath and all tensed up, and let loose another shot that struck the target in the lower leg.

"Holy shit," I was thinking, "I am really, really off today." Then I wondered if maybe I'd somehow gotten some bad ammunition. That happens. Maybe Mike was playing a prank on me and had put some damaged goods in my weapon. Funny what the excuse-making factory can produce.

The guy was still on his feet but had turned his back to us. I fired again and watched as his butt cheek exploded. He staggered but didn't fall.

"Hit him again! Hit him again!" I heard over the comms. At least one of my worries was eased. The assault team leader who was shouting encouragement to me had at least just verified that I wasn't missing—it was that this bastard wouldn't just die already.

I didn't know how this guy found the strength to do this or if he was like a beheaded chicken running around with just the last nerve impulses firing, but he started to run! He was heading deeper into the trees. I cracked another round, and I saw a tree branch jump and then fall. I had no idea if the round got the guy or not.

At that point, the platoon sergeant called it off. He wanted to send his guys in there to secure the weapon and to photo-document the two sure kills. I knew that I couldn't fight it, so I didn't say anything. I was sulking big-time, though. I hated missing. I was always really, really hard on myself, and instead of thinking about the two guys we'd taken down, and the rounds we'd put into the other guy, all I could think about was that I'd failed and that I'd let everyone down. I didn't even want to think about what the Tier 1 man was thinking.

Reluctantly, I joined the rest of the squad where the gun and the two bodies lay. I stood off to one side, not wanting to talk with anybody. At one point, Mack (a really hard-core dude who was at that point an assaulter, but who eventually became a sniper) said, "Hey, Irv. Come here. Look at this."

To the left of the two bodies, where the third guy who refused to die had been, was a dark area where blood had pooled temporarily. Leading away from that dark spot were smaller splotches of discolored earth. Then, on a leaf of a small plant, I saw what Mack had seen—a pink foam: heavily oxygenated blood from an arterial bleed. Most likely it didn't come from the guy's leg wound. The other shots he'd taken to the gut were too low to have gotten a lung. It had to have been the final round; maybe the bullet had glanced off that tree branch and hit him in the back. That would have gotten the lung and produced that kind of pink-foam bleeding. No other kind of wound would have.

"Holy crap." There was a pretty clear blood trail leading from that through the tree line and into the clearing just a few yards beyond that.

I booked it over to my platoon sergeant.

"I can track the guy. I can go get him. Finish him off if he's not dead. But he probably is. We can verify it."

He thought about it for a few seconds, then shook his head, "No good, Irv. Not worth it. He'll bleed out eventually. That's all that matters. We have to get moving again."

A couple of other guys chimed in, "Yeah, don't worry about it, Irv. We believe you. You hit him, right? That's all that matters."

"That was a Tier 2 display you put on, right? Couldn't dial it up any higher?"

"If I'm ever facing a firing squad, guys, please, please let Irv be the guy with the live round."

Their sarcasm was as thick and bubbly as the blood. I wasn't in the mood for it, but I couldn't help myself. I rose to the bait and told those trolls that I was sure I'd hit the guy. *Look at all the blood!*

They wouldn't give up, and as we moved out, they kept ragging me about how I'd messed up. It was all good-natured stuff, I knew. But I was hard on myself, and— there's that word again—"whining" a bit, amounting to an open invitation to the rest of the guys to give me crap. It eventually devolved into a "did-not-did-so" level of mature debate. But at least it got me talking and out of my pout-funk. In any case, nothing they could say to me was as bad as what I was thinking about myself.

After we'd stopped beating the maybe-not-dead-horse subject of my incompetence, the conversation turned to what we'd all seen: a guy who'd had multiple rounds put into him who seemed to possess superhuman strength.

I'd seen more than my share of that before. A lot of the bad guys we'd fought against were high on drugs. They felt no pain and also had so much adrenaline going through them that unless you took them out with a clean head shot, it would take as many as five or six, and sometimes more, rounds to bring them to the ground. I was about to launch into a story of seeing that while on an operation in Iraq as a machine gunner, but given how much crap was floating around among us all, I figured it was best to just keep my mouth shut or change the subject.

Turns out I didn't need to do anything to get everyone's attention focused on something other than my recent poor performance. We'd only gone about another thousand yards when I heard over the comms from the lead assault team, "Contact. Contact. Four targets ahead."

Mike and I were near the head of the line, and sure enough standing in the middle of the road were four Afghan bad guys. And I really mean bad guys. Each had his bandolier strapped across his chest, and their faces and heads, with the exception of the eyes, were wrapped in a black and gray kind of houndstooth-patterned *shemagh* (head scarf), knotted to the right side. They also wore what I always thought of as their hospital-pajama tops and bottoms—both in white. They were dressed exactly like the desert guys I'd seen in *National Geographic* and *Time* back in the day. It was weird to see them out in the open like that, but I wasn't going to question my luck. I figured I had the perfect opportunity to turn my bad luck around, restore my reputation, ease up on my self-criticism, and shut a few of our guys up.

Everyone else took a knee while Mike and I crawled to the lead. Mike was right alongside me as we prepared to set up shop.

"Let's work outside-inside."

"Got it." Mike crawled a few yards off to my right.

Everybody was in position to do this by the book. My platoon sergeant, Mack, was right behind me, ready to give the fire order. The assault team leader was off to my left. Alongside Mack was our radio operator, Mackey, ready to call up the body count to those higher up in the chain of command. The assault leader was responsible for laying down cover in case the bad guys returned fire. With our sniper weapons there'd be a bit of lag time between shots, so if after we got the Hajis on the outside of the cluster the two inside guys were fast and disciplined enough to turn on us, he'd distract them, or worse.

We were about four hundred yards from the targets. In training, we'd done three-hundred-yard targets without a scope, so this was a chip shot really, something well within easy range. I looked over at Mike and gave him a quick nod. He returned it. We were good to go. He'd take out the guy on the far right; I'd get the guy on the far left. We'd take the same sides on the two in the center.

Everything was so still that I could hear Mike take his weapon off safety. I heard the click of mine as I did the same. I eased my finger onto the trigger.

"Stand by," Mack said, "Let's get confirmation that we're clear to go hot."

I couldn't believe what I'd just heard. What? Clear to go hot? These guys were armed to the teeth. They looked like Afghan Rambos with that ammo strapped around their shoulders. And we have to stand by for confirmation? Confirmation of what? Was somebody going to go up to them and say, "Excuse me, guys, but we were wondering if you were planning to go out and kill anyone today? You are? Well, okay then, give us a sec and we'll try to figure something out."

In all fairness, Mack was doing the right thing by figuring out our options. Too often in Helmand Province we got into a run-and-gun cycle. By that I mean we'd go to one location and engage targets there, which would alert other bad guys in the area, so we'd have to engage again, and repeat that over and over throughout the duration of the operation. The more times you engaged the enemy, the more you were exposing your own guys to fire and increasing the chances of somebody getting hit.

We were out there to get after some high-value

targets—some key players in the Taliban. Maybe figuring out a way to go around these four guys would have made that simpler. Maybe if word came to these HVTs that Americans were nearby killing some of their troops, they'd decide to beat feet and leave their position (which we'd learned about through some hard and dangerous work) to live to fight another day.

I understood that, but I also understood this: If we let these guys go today, they'd live to fight another day. And that would maybe mean that they'd be part of some ambush on another unit, maybe one not as capable or as well armed or as well versed in this kind of fighting. Did it make sense, then, to give them a free pass today knowing that they could kill somebody else tomorrow? It was clear to me that they were prepared for a fight. Not just because of how they were kitted out, but based on the fact that they were standing in the open at an intersection. How many times had we had this kind of opportunity?

I lay on my belly considering all of this and felt my heart rate and blood pressure skyrocketing. My heartbeats were so rapid it felt like I was rising up off the ground with each one of them. To ease the strain of looking through my scope, I lifted my head a bit. The four guys were still there talking, framed by a few low buildings to either side of them.

I decided that I had to go back to basic sniper training principles, and focused on my breathing.

Deep breaths.

Deep breaths.

Deep breaths.

I could feel the effects, and now my heartbeats were still rapid, but I could feel the gaps in between them. That's when you want to squeeze the trigger—between the beats. "You want to be dead meat behind the gun" was the way one instructor in Sniper School had put it, with the only thing alive your trigger finger. That's kind of easy to do when you're aiming at a target, but when you're thinking that you're about to take another human's life—and you try really, really hard to not think about that at all—you add in another variable that gets your heart pumping and your mind unclear. You also can't think about the fact that your firing of your weapon is another way of giving away your position and drawing the attention of your enemy to your location.

In a way, I was glad that we were waiting for confirmation. It was helping me get my head, my heart, my lungs, and my eye together. I took the time to pull my scope all the way out to ten power, the highest magnification. I kept scanning the figure in front of me, relaying what I saw back to the platoon sergeant—the ammo belts, the sidearm, the AK47, the knife. I don't have to use the comms because Mack was right behind me and it's like I'm in an echo chamber, hearing him repeat what I said, vaguely hearing what's coming back to him over his comms like a low buzz of static.

At that point, I'd had enough. One of the guys moved and I was certain they were getting ready to leave, all four of them. I wasn't going to let them get away. I started to pull some slack out of the trigger. The higher-ups could do what they wanted to me, but I wasn't going to wake up in a few days and hear about how we'd lost one of our guys or some other guy and be left wondering if the guy who took him out was one of these four. I couldn't live with that.

"I'm going. I'm going," I whisper-hissed to Mike. I heard him make some indistinct sound of agreement, a kind of *mhmmnm* grunt.

Above that, I heard Mike's weapon creaking against the bipod as he pushed down on the Win Mag to absorb some of the recoil he knew he was about to feel.

"Hell yeah," I thought, "we are ready to rock and roll."

I had the slide almost out and was about to squeeze when I heard the first sounds of the word "clear" coming from Mack and I sent that round and watched as my guy collapsed. An instant later, just as planned, Mike's guy bit the dust.

Instinct and learning combined in those instants. When I was a kid, because my dad was in the military, I'd gotten ahold of a copy of the book *The Ultimate Sniper,* by John Plaster. At the time, and still today in some people's minds, it is *the* bible of sniping. Plaster stressed the idea of not becoming too target-fixated: Don't think of what you see in the scope as a full human body. Pick out something on that target—a button, a tear in the coat, or anything else that you see—as your aiming point.

I picked out a bullet on his left-side bandolier above the crux of the X—essentially, where his heart was located. That was what I hit: that exact bullet.

The two survivors took off running, my guy on the left racing toward a ditch. From behind, I heard the radio operator reporting in, "One down. Two down."

"Two to go," I thought.

Suddenly that number changed a bit. From the right a white car came screaming into the intersection, then turned right.

"Car! Car! Car!" I screamed.

"Roger. Tracking!" he shouted back.

That left me to take out the bad guy heading toward the ditch. With him running to my left and away from me, I didn't have a whole lot of time to take a bead on him. I just centered on his body and fired. He threw his hands up in the air kind of like he was signaling a touchdown and spun a bit before going down that shallow incline and out of sight.

From my right, I could hear Mike's Win Mag thundering as he went after the guy who'd jumped into the car. There was no way Mike could hear me, but my mind was full of instructions for him. He was just firing away, and I wanted him to take his time, to have some purpose for those shots. To go after the tires or the headrest.

I started to fire as well, but the car kept moving away.

Then I remembered the cars there have the driver's controls on the right and not the left. How stupid am I?

Mike must have done some damage to the vehicle or the driver, because it slowed and then came to a complete stop, its brake lights flashing on and then off and then on.

We started to push up this narrow alleyway, so narrow that we had to stay single file. I was out front, Mike behind me, an assaulter behind him. I had visions of us getting to the end of the alleyway and being spit out of some kind of pneumatic tube and being laid into by the guy who'd escaped, the one I'd wounded. Freaking scary.

Fortunately, our eyes in the sky were up and functioning, and they told us that nobody was out there waiting. We continued to walk and eventually made our way toward where the car had come to a stop. The vehicle was still running, but no driver seemed to be behind the wheel. The windshield was intact, though darkened by blood and viscera. As I got closer, I could see that the driver was slumped over. I knew he wasn't playing possum, because so much of him was spread across that glass. I could see a large impact wound, the white bone of his shoulder blade exposed and pointing like a turn signal. I'd seen a lot of dead guys in my years, but the amount of blood spattered inside that car's interior made me think that Mike had taken out ten guys, not just one.

I guess the adrenaline had drained out of me. A few

minutes ago I was superhyped and eager. Now I was feeling kind of down about the whole thing. Not that I'd missed, but that this guy was dead. The other two, and possibly a third one as well, were also dead. We'd done that to them.

I watched as the K-9 handler and his dog came up and did a quick search of the car. The dog indicated the car by barking, so one of the explosives guys popped the trunk while another opened a rear door. The back-seat had been removed, making the car into a kind of makeshift pickup truck. In that flat space was an arsenal of every kind of handheld weapon we faced over there—AKs, RPGs, sidearms. Suddenly I didn't feel so bad anymore. These guys had something big planned, and we'd wrecked it for them. Good on us.

I also walked along one flank of the car, the driver's side, the right side, and saw that it was dotted with exit and entrance holes. It was like Mike had been firing at it with magic bullets that wove in and out, trying to find the heart of the driver. That pattern was so un-usual we had the ID team take photos of it with their digitals.

We left all the weapons in the car and then torched it and tossed in a thermite grenade to make all of it use-less. Seeing all that go up in flames was as good as sitting around a fire with a bunch of guys drinking a few beers. We were all quiet as we stood there. Wasn't much to say at that point. We'd gotten no reports of there being any squirters, so it was time to continue moving on. We altered our route, so we switched things up and put the dog and his handler on the lead. That made me feel a little more comfortable, knowing that the dog was good at sniffing out explosives like IEDs.

While we were waiting for the dog to get some water, I heard one of the guys ask, "What the hell is that?"

He pointed up toward the power lines that spider-webbed all over the village.

"Mother—"

"A goddamn IED," one of the assaulters, Johnson, who had been with the unit since well before I'd joined it and had to be close to thirty-five or so, said with a mixture of appreciation and disgust.

"Somebody's been paying attention in class," Grimes added.

"Yeah, the Hajis have been," Mack said. He understood that over time, the various kinds of contractors, mercenaries, advisers, and whoever else had been coming to Helmand to aid them had been teaching them some new techniques. IEDs didn't have to be planted like mines; brush up against hanging ones and you got a similar effect. Hide them in the carcass of a dead animal, use remote control, rig entire houses. The longer we were there, the more advanced their techniques and tactics seemed to get. You don't want to wait too long to wipe them out.

For a long time guys worried about what it would be

like to have something blow up beneath them. How awful it would be to lose a foot, a leg, your junk. Now we had to wonder and worry about what it would be like to have shit come raining down from above. In a weird variation on what kids used to ask about "which would be worse," I'd heard guys talking about whether it would be better to be killed or really disabled. Messed up or dead? What about making it out alive and intact?

I stood there thinking about that for a few moments while the dog sat beneath that dangling IED and barked at it, alerting us, letting us all know that it was indeed an explosive device. I was used to seeing those dogs moving along with their noses to the ground; now were we going to have to train them to watch their twelve, to keep their heads up?

The call went out to the Explosive Ordnance Disposal crews to take care of it.

We still hadn't reached our objective. As we moved out, we got an answer to one of the questions that I had. All the commotion we'd stirred up hadn't, according to our command guys, alarmed our target enough for him to move. By this time we'd been out for more than six hours. The eastern horizon was beginning to grow light. We didn't have a whole lot of time to get to the objective and bring in this HVT.

Good thing that we didn't encounter anyone else as we made our way out of that first village or as we approached the second. Approximately two hundred yards from the target, we split off to take our positions. Mike and I climbed a roof of a building just south of the main objective: a low-slung house that, instead of having sharp corners, was all rounded, as if it had been rolled out of Play-Doh. We set up for overwatch and for the first time that night, I felt a bit of relief. Maybe because we were no longer on the move, maybe because we didn't encounter any bad guys on the way into the village, but I felt like I could just ease off the throttle a bit. I was eager for the assaulters to breach the door or do whatever else it took to get inside so I could fully relax.

Three hours into this operation, and I was really hurting for a cigarette. I'd brought along a pack, in defiance of regulation, and I stood there fingering its cellophane wrapper. My mom and dad never smoked, and when I was downrange, I kept pleading with them to send me some. My mom was adamant in refusing, telling me that it was a filthy habit and that if I wanted to smoke, well then, I should just walk down to the gas station on the corner and get them myself. I'd laugh at that and try to explain to her that where I was in Afghanistan, there were no 7-Elevens, no corner gas stations, no Wal-Marts. She said that was good, then maybe I'd break the habit, and that if not, I guess I'd just have to find another way.

I stood on the roof, smiling at the memory of the defiance in her voice. She was looking out for me and my best interests, and I was doing the same for the guys below me. They'd entered the building and all seemed quiet. A second later, I heard the *blip–blip–blip* of machine gun fire and saw muzzle flashes coming from inside a building adjacent to the objective. The third assault team was lighting some guy up and I could see the figure fleeing the house and entering a kind of courtyard and heading out into the fields surrounding the homes.

"Mike. Mike. Mike," I shouted, alerting him to the squirter, who was moving diagonally away from Mike's sector.

"I'm on him," I added a second after the alert.

I heard Mike's Win Mag fire and an instant after that I let a round go. The guy staggered a bit, from Mike's leg shot, and then his head seemed to explode as my round impacted him. That was a one-in-a-million lucky shot on my part. I barely had time to aim, and if he hadn't staggered I likely would have missed. I hadn't calculated anything, hadn't led him.

My attention returned to the squashed house. I could see flashes through the window, heard our guys yelling, "Get down! Get down!" in Pashto and a bunch of other people screaming, yelling, and crying. To my left, in the other building where the guy had come from, there was a second set of the same visuals and sounds. I then heard a bunch of dogs barking and out of the corner of my eye I saw some light glinting off of something. I turned and saw a woman come out of a house, and it was like she was wearing a sequined dress or something; light was catching various facets of it and shimmering. She's leading a kid by the hand, and the kid breaks free of her and starts to run. She didn't go after him, but stood there with her hands on her hips, and above all this other racket, I heard the most piercing sound I'd ever heard in my life. The kid froze in his tracks at the sound of his mom's voice.

The kid tentatively took a few steps back toward his mom, like he knew what was coming to him. Sure enough, she took him by one hand, and with the other swatted his backside till the kid was wailing. I started to laugh at the absurdity of all these goings-on. A simple in-and-out seizure of an HVT had turned into a kind of frantic three-ring circus. What was I supposed to look at? The dancing bears? The clowns? The lion tamer?

There was so much going on, but I had to do what I'd failed to do in taking out the guy I'd wounded—get back to the basics and focus.

The glittery lady reminded me of my mom and how she'd handle me like that when I was acting out.

My thoughts returned to the firefights. We were still in overwatch mode and I could see a bunch of activity in the town, shadows and figures heading our way. Mike was in contact with our ground force commander (GFC).

He was asking for permission to fire on a location. Don, the GFC, asked him about our range. Mike relayed his question: "He wants to know if we're good to a grand."

Even though it was growing lighter to the east, we were still in murky darkness. With night vision on we could see, at best, out to eight hundred yards and not the thousand yards Don was asking about. Given what we were dealing with, I thought six hundred was our max.

"Tell him we're good to mile." I was feeling cocky and added Don's thousand to the more realistic estimate of six hundred. At a mile, everything you'd see through the scope and the night vision would be grainy at best. I could see shapes but nothing that I could clearly identify as a weapon being carried or anything like that. At that point, I was really tired of the idea of requiring absolutely clear confirmation before firing. This whole place was filled with people trying to take us out and not asking questions; why should we?

Don appeared below us, "Anybody you see with a gun, out to a grand, a whole grid square, you take them out."

He must have read my mind. I was good with the weapon sighting and even better with the idea that we no longer had to wait for permission or for the bad guys to be right up on us. This was more like long-distance sniping and not direct action. Cool. Add that to the mix for this bizarre night in Helmand.

I could see that Mike shared my excitement at the prospect of taking out a few more guys that night. This was a night of firsts—the Tier 1 guy being with us, the chaplain, and now a commander issuing as close to a fire-at-will order as I'd ever heard.

I scanned the area below us. To my far left, I saw a portion of our assault team zigzagging their way toward where I'd fired on that single squirter. They were enclosing on him, I figured. I shined my laser out there and something flashed. I focused on that flash and sure enough, there was a guy lying with his back against a low berm with his hands in the air. They were shaking and every few seconds when our lights caught his left arm at just the right angle, it was like his wrist sparked. I realized that the guy was wearing some kind of watch. I don't know why, but that seemed odd to me. What was a Taliban guy doing with a watch?

I stayed focused on the downed and wounded guy, making sure that as the assaulters approached him, he didn't do anything stupid. The handler and the dog came sprinting toward them. I thought the dog was in attack mode, but they both just sprinted past the soon-to-be-prisoner toward the main objective.

"Sniper One. Watch this guy. Watch this guy. Out in the field, far left."

One of our guys had alerted me to something I hadn't noticed. From out of the darkness, an Afghan farmer came strolling out like he'd heard the commotion and wanted to see what was up. That never failed to amaze me. I'd seen this so many times, people just coming out of their homes or walking in from some other part of town to watch the firefight or whatever. I'd even seen a few people walk through the middle of a firing zone, flinching sometimes when a round zinged right past them, but otherwise just moseying along. This guy wasn't a moseyer but a spectator. He stopped on the road dividing the field from the village and squatted down to observe. He wasn't armed and seemed to pose no threat, so I fanned my vision away from him.

Our dog wasn't barking, but I could hear another canine going apeshit. I love dogs, but this dog's barking was out of control and one of those piercing, ear-ringing kinds of barks that is just so annoying. It sounded like it was very close. I looked down and he (at least I think it was a "he") stood with his head down and his butt in the air and his tail doing that cobra-like tail-twitching thing. I wanted to shoot that dog, and probably should have—he was giving away Mike's and my position. But I didn't have the heart to do that. I was looking for something to throw at him to scare him off. Also, the idea that he was alerting other people to our presence was kind of a joke. We'd had firing weapons and screaming and flash bombs and every other kind of noise for a while now. If you were sleeping through that, you probably didn't present any kind of threat.

At this point, in the small clearing between all the

buildings, we'd started to round up a bunch of Hajis. I didn't like that too much because when there's a big cluster like that, you've got us and the bad guys all mixed in together. I wanted a clear line of sight and line of fire on the bad guys, obviously, but that wasn't possible. The guys knew where Mike and I were positioned, but in the heat of all that was going on, it was hard to remember that point.

"Guys, can you part the sea?"

That expression is just what you think. The assaulters are trained to make a more orderly configuration so that we can better identify who's who, or who's on what team, and clear some space. That separation makes it a lot easier for me. One of my pet peeves was when guys forgot to do that. I also hated it when somebody was hot-miking, and in all the confusion that night, a lot of that was going on. Guys left their microphones on and that meant that rest of us were hearing everything they said, their breathing, if they blew snot out of their noses, spit, chewed gum. All of it added to the chaos.

This time, though, I was glad that nobody had yelled at the guy to turn off his switch. I could hear our guys yelling at the prisoners, a group of a dozen or more, demanding that they get down on their knees, their bellies, or their backs.

I recognized Ramirez's voice. I picked him out of the crowd and saw that he was standing face-to-face with one the prisoners. I scoped them both and I could see the bad guy and he was smiling even as Ramirez shouted at him and gestured at the ground with his weapon, trying to get the guy to go down. I also watched as the guy started to take his left hand down from over his head toward his chest.

"Holy shit," I thought, "the guy's got on a suicide vest."

I wasn't the only one who thought so. One of the platoon leaders, named Adams, started yelling, "Hands up! Hands up!" He was gesturing what he wanted the guy to do, but the prisoner just kept smiling, and then he started to laugh.

"No! No! No!" Adams shouted at him.

The guy didn't move but just kept smiling and then he said, as clear as anybody could have said it, "Fuck you."

Our guys stepped back, clearing my lane even more, and I fired. The first round kind of deflated him, and he sagged a bit and went limp. At that, a bunch of our guys opened up on him from close range. He was lying on the ground and I could see dirt clods and dust being kicked up all around him. I focused again and let the guys know that I was about to send another round into him, just to be sure. It found its home and the guys confirmed that he was dead with a couple of raised thumbs.

Only later did I really think about how much those guys trusted me. There was a four- to five-foot alley for me to shoot into. The guys just stood there and waited for me to deliver that killing round, trusting that I wouldn't flinch or throw off the round some other way and take one of them out. Only an hour or so earlier, they'd been giving me crap about the one that got away. That's the way it was with my brothers and me, kicking and scratching and barking at each other like angry dogs, then a while later acting like nothing at all bad had gone down between us. If I could bottle that feeling of satisfaction and camaraderie and sell it, I'd be a very, very wealthy man and there'd be no need for anybody to ever stick a heroin needle in their arm.

All the craziness had settled down a bit, and we were back in our routine. Mack's voice came over my comms, resuming his natural conversational tone, kind of like an airline pilot updating flight status: "I think we've got everything we needed here. Time for us to get up and go." He relayed the new coordinates for our extraction point and I watched as the rest of the units all formed up for the walk out of there.

Mike and I continued our overwatch, waiting to see the backs of the last of our guys before dismounting that roof. From that vantage point, I could see the house we'd originally been sent to; there was still a bit of commotion there. I could hear an Afghan guy screaming and crying. I wondered where the Tier 1 guy was. I hadn't seen him for quite a while. I scanned the line of our guys heading to the extraction point, but didn't see him anywhere.

I'd told Mike to let me know when the rest of the guys were about a hundred yards outside the village. He let out a short, sharp whistle to signal me, and we soon caught up with them. I was always aware of how vulnerable we were when we mounted up inside the helicopters, so Mike and I took positions on the far sides of the landing zone and waited for everybody but the commander and Mack to be aboard before we ran up the ramps ourselves.

You might expect that it might be like a victorious locker room after going through a hellish night like that.

It wasn't.

We were all pretty tired and lost in our own thoughts, so it was quiet all the way back and even when we passed through that gates and inside the wire. As we were about to climb off the minibus, Mack stood up and said, "Team leaders in the debrief room now."

We went through the usual routine of everybody reporting back on what they saw and did, including listing the kills, so that the after action report could be compiled. I learned one thing that disturbed me. Some of the ruckus that had gone on inside the main objective had to do with the military working dog (MWD) assigned to us. Panzer was a cool dog, a Belgian Malinois who, unlike some of the other MWDs I'd worked alongside, was pretty cool about letting people besides his handler interact with him. That dog was as lean and fit and ferocious on command as any of the rest of them, but he seemed kind of chill when not at work, as most of us were.

When Panzer went inside that building, he must have freaked out one of the residents, who cut him with a knife. To show you how well trained and cool that dog was, even though he was being attacked, he didn't take that woman out. He was still on his leash and the handler and a couple of other guys were trying to disarm her. You have to remember that even though we all had our armor on and it could stop a bullet, it didn't offer the same kind of protection from a blade. They kept trying to get her to drop the big old knife she had, but she was just so freaking out and so intent on doing more damage to the dog that she wouldn't listen to any of us, the interpreter, or whatever common sense she might have had. None of the assaulters wanted to do it, but eventually someone had to put a round into her to end the threat and her life. I heard about that in the debrief, along with the fact that Panzer had to be taken to the medical unit to be stitched up but was otherwise going to be fine in a few days.

Having to shoot a woman wasn't any easy thing for anybody to do, and it was absolutely the last resort in that situation. We had to receive clearance in order to do it. I didn't even want to know who the guy who had to do the shooting was, and nobody really ever talked about it except to say how fucked up that whole situation was for everybody involved—the shooter, the victim, her family, the dog.

One thing that troubled me was my thoughts about whether or not to take out that other dog, and also how in our debrief, the commander said something that he saw as being messed up. Our MWDs were considered to be like a piece of equipment—a weapon, a vehicle, somebody's freaking office chair—and it had to be reported on as being damaged.

Not wounded.

Not injured.

Damaged.

We all sat there shaking our heads. We all knew that a bunch of times, the dogs were the first ones inside an objective after an entrance had been briefed, risking taking fire. They'd detected a bunch of IEDs that saved lives or limbs. They were a big part of our unit and of our lives. Panzer and other dogs helped make us feel a little bit more like regular guys who had a dangerous job. We'd be out there killing bad guys and then come back inside the wire and laugh and joke around with Panzer, throw him a tennis ball, and ooh and aah as he jumped and twisted in the air to catch it. We'd give each other crap when we lost at tug-of-war to the furry dude.

We were all brothers in arms, the four-legged among

us and the two-legged. I've heard people say that one of the great things about dogs is that they live in the moment; they don't think about the past or the future. I'm not so sure about that, because every dog I've had and known seems to understand when chow time is coming up. But you get the point.

It was weird to come back from an operation like the one we had and have guys split off to go to PT in the gym, some to shower, some to go eat, some to make phone calls home, or some to rack out. We treated what we did as just another day at the office, didn't talk much about it after, and got ready the next day to do it all over again. We weren't treated like a line item in a budget, but that's how we had to look at the killing and the injuring we did to the enemy.

Account for it.

Note it.

Move on.

The other takeaway from that experience was simple. I was thinking so much about the Tier 1 guy and my "audition" that I lost my focus for a bit out there. Instead of concentrating on the job that I had to do in taking out that bad guy who didn't seem to want to die, I was thinking about the job that I wanted to have next. That wasn't good. I got away with it, but I had to figure out a way to keep my desire to be perfect from getting in the way of me doing my job effectively. I was still learning and still growing. Funny thing is, in all the commotion that was going on, I, and everybody else, lost track of the Tier 1 guy. He just seemed to disappear. How cool was that?

SIX

WITHOUT REMORSE

"IRV! LET GO of your junk, man. You're out in public!"

The rest of the forty-man 1st Platoon who heard Ramirez's successful attempt to punk me laughed. I felt my ears burning with embarrassment, but there was no way I was taking my hands from my groin. We were just outside of Kandahar in the late fall of 2008 before the surge that President Obama instituted. We may have been crossing a relatively small pond, waist-deep in water the color of feces, but in my mind, I was back home in Texas sitting on a couch a similar color to that water watching television.

I was home for a while between deployments. Jessica was at work and I had the day to myself to fill with whatever diversion I could find. That meant TV, and in this case a show on Animal Planet called *Monsters Inside Me*. This documentary about infectious diseases fascinated me. I wasn't a hygiene freak then or now, but something about how these tiny little microorganisms wreak huge havoc on the human body kind of appealed to me. Talk about your "Without hesitation; without remorse" kind of creatures. These things were relentless and lived to kill and destroy.

The particular episode I was thinking of when I stood on the bank of that filthy bit of water was about a particularly nasty microscopic dude that could flow up your urethra when you peed while submerged in water. It would get up inside you and start to destroy your organs. If you didn't get help, you'd die. I wasn't about to piss in the water, but I wasn't taking any chances, so I had my hand clamped pretty firmly on my groin. If I could help it, there wasn't a single thing working its way up into me.

It wasn't just the TV show that had me freaked out about sanitation and disease. We had to take pills, make sure we drank clean water, and do all kinds of other things to protect ourselves. A few years before this I was reminded of how dangerous Iraq and Afghanistan could be without even being shot at or having an explosive device detonated near you. This happened during the operation in Iraq I already told you about—the one with the large building where we came under attack. The one we referred to as the Hotel Party.

What I didn't tell you is that on that operation, one of the mechanics who maintained a bunch of different vehicles was nearing the end of his deployment. He was thinking that maybe this would be the end of his Army days, too. He wasn't sure if he wanted to re-up, but he knew that he didn't want to have his career end without him getting a chance to see what life was like outside the wire. He volunteered to go on a ride-along on that operation. You know how crazy that whole thing got. What I didn't tell you is that even before we got to that hotel party, we had to skirt around a cesspool. Not everywhere in Iraq, but in too many places, open sewage flowed through the streets or sewers emptied into these nasty, nasty pools.

I'm not exactly sure what, I'll call him Q, was thinking. but as we approached one of them, he wound up in it instead of going around it. I don't know if he thought it was a puddle or he had his head on high-speed swivel due to being new at this, but I saw him floundering around in that cesspool. A few guys jumped in to help pull Q out of there. He had staggered and fallen, and it was clear that he'd swallowed some of the water and sludge. He was hacking and coughing and spluttering, trying to spit that stuff out of his mouth. I stood there staring at him, and it was kind of funny in a way. Here he is wanting to get a taste of the combat life and he got a taste of something most of us had never had. I also felt really bad for him, too, because after you stop that first instinctive laughter, you realize that this guy is in a world of hurt. I didn't know how bad, but I saw that he was being led to the medical vehicle, and they hauled ass out of there. I didn't see Q for a while, but the guys had heard that he was taken to the compound's infirmary and things were looking rough for him.

A couple of days later, I saw Q sitting outside one of the housing units. He was all wrapped up in a blanket. I stubbed out my cigarette and walked over to him.

"What's up, Q? How're you doing?"

He shook his head and looked up at me. I could see that his eyes had turned yellowy. "Not so good, Irv. I'm getting out of here sooner than I thought, though."

He went on to explain that the bacteria in the cesspool had done a number on him. His kidneys had nearly failed. He was on all kinds of antibiotics and was doing better now, but he was being medically discharged.

I really felt like, well, like shit for laughing at what I'd seen. Anytime anybody fell, with the exception of the time that Mike fell down that huge hole and broke his leg, you kind of laughed, as much out of surprise than anything. Human nature, I guess.

So, there I was outside Kandahar, trying to walk across that pond in penis protection mode, shuffling my feet along. I'd see pictures and scenes in movies of guys doing water crossing with their weapons held in hands extended above their heads looking all Rambo-like. I didn't care what I looked like or how slow I was walking or how wet the stock of my weapon was getting. I was thinking about some of the other adages and creeds that snipers preached—"One shot, one kill," for example—and thinking about how they might apply here. "Unseen but deadly" wasn't one of them, but I was thinking of adding that to my own personal list.

A mile or so beyond the water crossing, we came up on our objective. The briefing was one that they could have filmed months ago and shown over and over. High-value target. In-and-out. Time-sensitive. Sniper One will position himself here. Sniper Two there. Carrying five mags of .308 ammo. Yadda. Yadda. Insha'allah. Yadda.

I don't want to make it seem like I was checking out completely from those mission briefings. I was paying attention, but because we were essentially saying and then doing many of the same things on each of those operations, there was frequently little to distinguish one from another. Most of the time, those operations in 2008 went off without a hitch. We liked that, but just as I really like to eat Doritos, if I ate them all day every day as a snack, I'd get to the point where I wasn't noticing every nuance of what they tasted like. Mike and I took up our position on a rooftop across from the objective. The guys made their way inside quickly and without incident. Without anything much to do, Mike and I sat back to back, each of us using the other as a backrest.

"You going to keep driving that Grand Marquis when you get home for good?" Mike asked.

"Like to get rid of it."

"Thing's as big as my house," Mike snorted.

"I'd like to get a Harley," I told him. "Always wanted to ride."

"You kidding me? Your mom will whip your ass for doing that. Not to mention what Jessica will do."

I thought about that for a minute. Despite my earlier feeling that I'd been guilty of oversharing with Mike, as our relationship deepened I'd told him more about my mom and my wife. He liked both of them and they liked him. They knew that he was doing his best to help keep me safe.

What he was saying about my mom was true. She wasn't so much of a worrywart as she was a large worry bubble. Her anxieties would inflate and deflate a little bit, but mostly they were a constant source of pressure on me, on her, and—I had to imagine, though he didn't say as much—on my dad. I knew that my being overseas was a huge stress on her and on Jessica. That was why I was thinking that maybe it was time for me to call it quits. Still, there was a part of me that didn't want to call it quits, or at least not unless it was on my own terms. I was kind of caught in the "no remorse" aspect of the sniper's code, applying it to other parts of my career.

"I'd tell her it was a trade-off. I could come home and ride a motorcycle or keep adding on to my number of deployments." I didn't like the idea of worrying my mom any more than I already had. I was pretty sure that she wasn't dealing with just regular old worry; based on my conversations with her, I'd started to have the feeling that it went deeper and was more serious than that. I wondered for a moment what my six deployments had done to me, let alone what effect they were having on my wife and my mother.

My conversation with Mike was interrupted by some intel on the comms. We learned that on our exfiltration (exfil) route, the eyes in the skies had picked up some of the enemy taking up positions along it.

"Oh, man, here we go again."

"As my moms used to say," Mike began, and then paused before adding, "if it was easy . . ."

But that was exactly what I was hoping it would be. No shots fired. Helicopter ride back home. Eat chow. Watch a few DVDs with the guys, get some sleep.

"No rest for the wicked," Mike said.

"Roger that," I added.

And to be honest, we all needed some rest. Getting shot at was no fun. I enjoyed doing the shooting, but the converse wasn't true. As much as it was physically possible, my body had adapted to the inverted hours we kept—sleep during the day, work at night. What was most in need of rest was my mind. Keeping your situational awareness at its peak was one thing; having to remember the plan of action was another; having to adapt, adopt, and revise again and again was the most taxing of all.

As Mike and I packed our gear, I tried to visualize the maps we'd been shown. Our exfil route was north of the objective along what passed for a major route through this town. The helicopters would be landing on the outskirts of the town in a field bordered by a couple of freestanding buildings.

At no point during the brief did anybody talk about the armed resistance we were now likely to meet as we made our way to the original exfil route and along it. How we get out of there, then, was for us to decide, with assistance from above. I had a route in mind but knew that it was up to the commander to make the call. I always liked knowing where I was going and being at the head of the pack, then trailing along at the rear. For that reason, I told Mike that once we got down, we'd take a position behind the first assault team's point man.

I don't know if I would have liked, or would have had the skill set, to be one of the point men. Not only did they have to have their eyes scanning all around them, they also had to keep their eyes on their GPS device to make certain they were leading us along the correct route. The easiest comparison I can make is, imagine driving in a city with your GPS monitor on your dash. You can't hear the GPS calling out directions. All you can do is see the highlighted route you're supposed to be on. You're looking at that screen but also having to pay attention to the other vehicles, pedestrians, the traffic signals. Now imagine doing all that while wondering if the next building you pass, the car that comes alongside you, has armed bad guys in it who want to shoot you.

Add to that, you're trying to listen to something important coming over the radio. In this case, we kept hearing that our comms experts had intercepted enemy radio transmissions revealing that they were aware of our presence and were tracking us. Once we left the more inhabited town area, we set out along a narrow footpath. I was on edge, because these bad guys had gotten smarter as time went on. They knew that we often came in on foot, and so they'd started to plant IEDs along the nonvehicular access routes.

A lot of times, we'd encounter the enemy without having advanced notification of their presence. In a way, that was better than this. We knew that these guys were out there; it was more a question of *when and where* we'd make contact than *if. If* was a constant. You were used to having that weight and worry on you. The *when and where* was a bit different. You kind of carried that in a different place. As a result, you noticed it more.

We were doing everything we could to stay safe— keeping out of the villages themselves, avoiding the water-filled ditches and dried riverbeds and high-traffic areas. We slowed our pace. At one point, platoon sergeant

Mack had us stop. We were in a fairly open position with just a couple of low outbuildings, hut-type structures that dotted the terrain. If there was a large enemy presence around, it would have been difficult for them to have found any hides.

"Can you guys see anything?" he asked.

I brought my scope up to my eye and began scanning. Mike did the same. All along our exfil route, we'd all been doing target detection. On an operation you were always on the lookout for anything that might give you a clue as to where a bad guy might be, where a booby trap might be waiting, anything out of the ordinary that could be a potential hide or a threat. You check every window and doorway. You look for anything that might seem out of place, what doesn't make sense, doesn't fit into the pattern of the environment.

At our halt, I ratcheted things up a bit. I started to do the tried-and-true, "If I Was a Sniper" test, attempting to discover a spot that I would have used if the roles were reversed. Again, we were in an area that was so sparse, it was hard to believe that anybody could be out there.

"I've got nothing," I reported to Mack.

"Negative," Mike added.

"Let's move," Mack said.

We crept along for another quarter mile before Mack halted us again. I went to a knee and started to scope. I spotted movement and then detected a small group of men less than a quarter mile from our position. It was difficult to determine the number of them because they were all dressed nearly alike and were moving back and forth between a house and a small open field. They'd do something inside the house and then come back out a minute or so later. They appeared to be unarmed, but I'd seen more than a few instances of guys like these carrying their weapons beneath their clothes.

Also, they'd frequently keep their weapons stashed out in a field. They'd appear to be just going on about their business, doing their farmwork, and then the next thing you knew they'd be firing at your position. Sometimes they'd take a few potshots at us, hide the weapon, and resume their farming activities. When we'd come up on them to question them, of course, they'd say that they weren't doing anything wrong. Given the ROEs, without absolute confirmation that it was that exact guy with the weapon, there wasn't much we could do except be grateful that nobody got hit.

Once we determined that it was likely safe to proceed, we resumed our walk out to the choppers. I hung back, continuing to monitor those men as the rest of the unit made its way past them. Once the lead guys were parallel to them, Mike and I hustled to the middle of the pack, again to provide cover for the guys in the back of the pack. To that point, all was good. After we'd all gone past them, I noticed the men in the field moving in a way that they hadn't before. They kind of ducked their heads away from us, and one of them brought his hands up to his face. To me, it looked like he was using some kind of communication device.

We always joked about the need to have your Spidey Sense, like Spider-Man did, that allowed you to pick up signals when something bad was about to go down. I got that feeling a few seconds after we'd all moved just beyond their position. The thought that something wasn't quite right no sooner flashed through my mind than I heard the sound of rounds snapping above our heads. Imagine what it sounds like when someone snaps their fingers, only continuously and faster than humanly possibly—*snapsnapsnapsnapsnapsnapsnapsnapsnapsnap*.

Whoever was firing that weapon had us in a good position. It was like he had an alley he could aim down with an open field to our left and a thin, silvered strip of a running stream to our right. We had very little nearby that we could take any kind of effective cover behind. I could feel the inside of my cheek sticking to my teeth. I realized it had been a couple of hours since I'd taken a drink. Though it wasn't hot yet, being slightly dehydrated was not good. I could almost feel my thoughts thickening as they moved through my sludgy brain. I had to free them up somehow, but taking the time to drink wasn't going to work at that point. I took in a few deep breaths and exhaled forcefully, trying to add some spark to ignite my thoughts about our next steps.

Everybody had dropped to the ground. I could tell that the rounds weren't just coming in high, but were coming in from an angle well above our position. They were firing high and long, the rounds kicking up dust storms on the track we'd come in on, maybe fifty yards behind us.

"Ditch the ladder, Mike," I told him. We needed to be as quick and mobile as possible.

I pressed my comms button and told the guys, "We're moving. We're moving."

As we set off, I heard the guys out front, the first assault team, begin to lay down suppressive fire for us.

Back in the day when I played youth league football, we had a coach who was a Vietnam vet and had become a physical education teacher. He was as old school as it gets. He used to make us do this drill he called the Duck Walk. You squat down, drop your butt nearly to the ground, bend your elbows and lift your arms like you had flapping wings, and do laps around the entire field. It was supposed to build up your legs, but it was torture on your knees. Mike and I had to do our version of that Duck Walk as we made our way past our prone comrades. It was agonizing, but no way were we going to raise our bodies up any higher than necessary. Using our outstretched hands to stabilize ourselves, sometimes dragging body parts and high-centering ourselves momentarily as we crawled over the other guys, we made our way to the front.

Because of how we'd been pinned down, the only ones who could fire effectively and not hit our own guys was the first assault team. That wasn't good, and we all knew it. Mike and I took a position just to the right of those guys, laying down along a very shallow incline, no more than two or three degrees, that led to the stream. I wriggled into the prone position, trying to work my way past the sharp rocks that jabbed at my thighs and elbows.

Through the scope I could see the faintest of sparks coming from the muzzle of a weapon positioned a few hundred yards from where our farmer friends had been standing. After I sighted on those sparks, I figured that most likely they were coming from an RPK machine gun; I could make out the hundred-round-capacity drum magazine. I also figured that they were closer to a third of a mile away, about five hundred meters, and not the quarter of a mile I'd first estimated. I was able to clearly identify three targets. One bad guy was behind the gun doing the firing. Another was crouched just above the first, giving him aiming and leveling directions, most likely.

The shooter and the aimer were positioned at the corner of a small building. They'd set up their firing position between two small structures, and the third guy was darting from one of them to the other and then back again. I couldn't figure out what the hell he was doing running these five-yard sprints back and forth like the print head on those old dot matrix printers we'd had in junior high. The sound of their weapon firing added to the impression. I hated that sound back then, and I wanted to eliminate it now and stop that crazy shit from running like that. Having something move in and out of your scope throws off your visuals, and is just plain irritating.

"Dude," I said to Mike, "just take that runner out." It was a tough shot from that distance and with the guy just being visible for a second or so at a time. To make it, you had to do what we call "trapping." You've probably seen videos of people shooting skeet—clay targets. When they move the barrel of the weapon continuously and pull the trigger while the gun is still in motion, that's called "tracking." The technique Mike had to use was trapping. You set your weapon up and aim at a fixed point and don't move the barrel of the weapon or any other part of it except the trigger. You look through your reticule, identify one point at one edge of the scope's field of vision, and a second point within that same field. Basically what you're doing is estimating when to fire so that the object moving through that line of sight will be centered as the round reaches that distance. Given this set of conditions, Mike was using a 3.5-mil lead so that the round would reach the bad guy two seconds after he released it. Essentially, the round would impact the target when he reached the center crosshairs within the scope. Simply put, you're making the target run into the bullet's path.

Mike's Win Mag was booming away. That thing was so freaking loud, even with my ear protection in, I felt like each discharge was hammering away at my eardrums. I was also firing rounds at the shooter and his aide. In situations like this, at least for me, the old saying "One shot, one kill" was just that—a saying. The Army preached it in training, but I learned that in combat, it took a lot more shots than just one to bring a guy down. When you can get in the prone position and really set up and take your time, sure, you can get very, very close to or actually achieve 100 percent accuracy and have "One shot, one kill" become a reality. But when you've got enemy fire coming into your position, and you're scrambling as quick as you can to eliminate that threat to your guys, things are lot more fluid, and chaotic, than that.

Firing from the prone position increases your chances of making that "One shot, one kill" work, but in my experience, I probably had to fire from a knee or from a rooftop ledge or from some other unorthodox and uncomfortable position close to three out of four times. Eventually, I talked with some of the higher-ups about sniper training and told them about my experience and how the training needed to be adapted so that guys were firing from positions they'd actually be in during a firefight.

Also, in this case, even though I was a sniper and wanted the kill, I realized that given how difficult my shot was, I'd be better off firing rounds like I was laying down suppressive fire than I would be sniping. I could barely make out the weapon and had a faint view of the two human figures, but they were tucked behind the leading edge of that wall just enough that my angle was too shallow to get around it. So from that distance and angle it was unlikely I could hit them; I had a better chance of hitting the building near them and maybe spraying them with the shrapnel that came off the building, temporarily obstructing their vision with dust, plain old distracting and worrying them. Then, if they were preoccupied with thoughts about where I was at and what might happen to them, one of the assault teams could flank those three guys, have a clearer shot at them and take them out themselves. I wasn't there to add to my personal tally. I was there to help get us all out of there alive, no matter what it took.

I kept firing rounds and so did Mike, and then at one point the runner did something really, really odd. He stopped his sprints and took a few steps closer to us and lay down in the path that led from where the other farmer/informers had been to where the gunners had set up. I started to wonder if this guy had been convinced to act as a decoy. It was like this was a carnival attraction or something; he was on some kind of chain that dragged him back and forth between those two buildings, and the machine broke down, or else he got so tired from running that he decided to just collapse right there and let us take him out.

I didn't fire on him and neither did Mike. I told Mike to fire his rounds at the gunners. I figured that his heavier rounds stood a better chance of penetrating that building and maybe we'd get lucky and take out those two other guys.

As if some telepathic cease-fire had been ordered, all of us on both sides stopped shooting. A weird silence came over the area. Smoke from the weapons fire drifted past on the predawn breeze. From my radio, I had heard that our second assault team was moving to the east— to the side opposite the stream—in order to flank the gunners. I wondered for a minute if maybe Mike or I had gotten incredibly lucky and struck the bad guys behind the building.

For some reason that I'll never understand, the two guys who'd enjoyed that protected position decided to abandon it. They stood up, the gunner taking some time to collapse the weapon's bipod, and they ran forward, looking like they wanted to join their motionless buddy in the middle of the road. I now had a clear shot on the gunner and "One shot, one kill" was in effect. My round struck him in the chest, lifted him off his feet, and twisted him in the air. The RPK hit barrel-first and then lay with its magazine up in the low grass.

Shots being fired from my far left caught my attention. One of our assault teams was laying down heavy fire on the second of the two buildings the runner had been dashing between. We started to receive fire from that position, and I realized that there were more than just those three guys out there. Why hadn't they fired on us before? Was the runner delivering messages back and forth between their two shooters? What the hell kind of strategy did these guys use?

After a minute that brief firefight extinguished itself.

We still had the runner-turned-lier in the middle of the road. I asked Pemberton if he'd hit him, but Mike couldn't confirm that. The third guy, the aimer, had tried to take cover briefly but then decided to go after the RPK. He grabbed the weapon, took a knee, and prepared to fire on us. He was making some adjustments to it, and that gave me enough time to trap him. I fired a round just to his left, between him and his original position behind the right-side building. That was my way of letting him know he could run but he couldn't hide. When the round kicked up dirt a few yards from him, he twitched and pulled back a bit, kind of like when you touch a light switch after static electricity has built up in you.

He continued to fumble with the gun and I took him out cleanly in the upper chest. Mike got him with another round as well, striking him in the lower back. I was good with that. Making sure that guy was dead was a good thing.

At that point we all received a cease-fire command. We were going to take what we call a "tactical pause." Everybody figured that we'd taken out all the bad guys by this point. We were spread around the area. One assault team had flanked to the west—the guys who had taken out the second shooter. Another had flanked to the east. They hadn't had to fire, since the gunner and aimer had decided to move forward and take us on in a frontal assault. The first assault team all stood up. It looked like the area was on fire. The machine guns, the large rounds from Mike's no-muzzle Win Mag, and the enemy's RPK had kicked up a huge amount of smoke and dust. Though my night vision, it looked like we were all on the surface of the moon, like we'd just stepped out of our lunar lander and were adjusting to the lighter gravity and the dust that rose higher than back on Earth.

I looked around and watched as guys started to swap out mags, and that pause kind of turned into a sigh, a huge exhale after all the craziness that had just gone on. I could still feel the tension in my neck and shoulders and jaw. I was still on the ground, still scanning. Right in the center of this were the three bad guys we'd taken out. The weapon was in the middle of them and they were splayed out like the different elements of a multitool—the screwdriver, the knife, the corkscrew.

All of a sudden, one of those three, the corkscrew, straightened itself and sprang into the air. It was like watching a Mixed Martial Arts fighter popping up off the canvas, a Haji Ronda Rousey. From somewhere, he produced a weapon, and I don't know how I did this, but I was so startled by the sight of this man jumping up after we'd all assumed he was dead, I squeezed the trigger on instinct. The bullet struck him in the thigh; I could see the hole in the fabric of his robes and hear the meat-smack sound of it going into his flesh. His facial expression didn't change—hard to believe after taking a .308 round in the leg; he didn't even stagger. He just lowered himself into a squat, like I'd seen lots of people from the East do when they were relaxing. He laid the weapon across his upper legs, covering his wound, and took one of his hands and brought it up to his chin, with his elbow resting on the stock of the AK he'd magically produced.

He'd gone from the runner to the possum to the squatter, and now he was there like *The Thinker*. He looked over toward me, and through the scope I could see him squinting. He was an older guy, judging by the folds and wrinkles around his eyes. I swear he was looking at me and thinking, "So, okay, are you going to shoot me or what?"

I'd done all that training and had been instructed in target fixation, and without warning or regret, something passed through me that had never before factored into my life as a sniper or soldier. I had this creeping belief that this was a variation on suicide by cop. All along this guy had been hoping that we'd end his life. He'd given us every opportunity, had wanted to make it difficult for us so that we wouldn't feel so bad. We'd kind of messed up those other opportunities and now there we were, looking across a space that was no more than a few hundred yards but might have been millions of miles given where he came from and what he'd seen and what he'd lived through.

"You got him?" Mike shouted, ending my seconds-long tactical pause.

"Yeah, man. Wait one."

The one turned into a two and then a three and then a four and then a five.

"What the hell," Mike said, his voice gone soft and confused. "I'm about to shoot this guy." His statement tailed off into a semi-question.

"All right. All right?" I said, my throat seared and the words sounding foreign. "Sending. Sending. Sending."

The guy never moved the whole time I had him in my sights until my round blew him back. The impact sent his legs flying toward me; one of his sandals spun in the air. The back of his head hit the ground, bounced slightly, and settled.

"Good shot. Good shot." Mike said, though with none of the enthusiasm he'd frequently display.

Mack was on the radio. "Everything good up there?"

I didn't want to consider all the different ways I could have interpreted "good," didn't have the vocabulary to express all the questions I had for him and the universe.

I resorted to the tried and true—"Roger that"—firing off a response out of instinct and hoping that it would find its way home, be a tracer I could follow to some safe place, guide me to a spot where warnings and re-morse had no role.

"We're moving," Mack said.

I stood up and dusted myself off. I took out a bandanna and cleaned my scope, lightly dusting it off so I wouldn't scratch. I took off my night vision, hoping that I'd be able to see more clearly what choices had been presented to me and the ones I'd opted to take.

"We'll cover you," I said to Mack as I nodded at Mike. He stepped forward as if to put his hand on my shoulder. He didn't, but he did grab the hose coming from my CamelBak hydration pack.

"You look like you could use a drink, brother," he said, his eyes locked on mine. I had to break that contact, but I did take in a good long draw from that mouthpiece, not minding one bit that it tasted of dust and warmth and night in Helmand.

Minutes later, in the chopper, I sat there thinking more about what had just happened. I wasn't sure if that man had come along to teach me a lesson. I'd never had somebody stare down that scope right at me. It was like he was assessing me and taunting me and pleading with me all at once. For a long time, I'd thought that the Afghans we took on weren't really fully human. I thought they were stupid, primitive people who chose to live a life with standards of decency and humanity far below our own. I knew that it helped me to do my job as a sniper to consider them as nothing more than a target.

Though we didn't exchange a word, it was like the two of us had had a conversation. In my mind, he'd given me the okay to do what it was I had to do. I have no idea if he had any intention of firing that weapon on us or not. He was armed. He'd made no indication that he wanted to surrender. He posed a lethal threat to us.

When racked out later that day after returning, I had a dream in which the two of us did exchange words. I'd never dreamed about combat before, but this one was vivid. I woke up from it with the man's words echoing in my head: "Are you going to do it or what?"

For the first time, I did feel remorse. I told Mike that I did, but I kind of joked about it, telling him that I'd violated the code and he should report me.

When I first heard the words "Without warning; without remorse," I didn't realize that remorse could ambush me without warning. I didn't understand that remorse wasn't a simple black-and-white, yes-or-no, good-or-bad thing. It had certainly been presented to me in that way. And I wondered now and for a long time after if my feeling remorse meant I should yes, be a sniper, or no, go back home. Was I a good soldier or a bad soldier? Harder still, I had one question that I pushed out of my mind until after I'd decided to leave the Army and began finding comfort and courage in the bottom of too many bottles of booze to not stay in my hide and assault it head-on: Was I good man or a bad man?

SEVEN

KEEPING TRACK OF YOURSELF

TEAM CHEMISTRY IS AN important part of success. I've read about football teams that won Super Bowls because all of the guys got along really well and they were a cohesive unit with all of their eyes focused on the same prize. Egos didn't get in the way, and they had the "next man up" attitude if an injury took out one of the starters. I've also read that some teams have won Super Bowls even though guys didn't get along—the defense thought the offense wasn't pulling their weight, the coaches of those two units didn't really talk to one another, and the guys fought each other as much as they fought the opposing teams. In both cases, they had something that sparked the fire in their bellies and they had the talent to overcome any kind of dysfunction. Or maybe things just rolled their way and Lady Luck was on their side.

All I know is that in my experience at war, team chemistry did matter—not so much in how guys interacted in the ready rooms or back home on the ranges, but definitely on the battlefield. You had to mesh and do your job regardless of how you might have felt about some of the other members of your team and their personalities.

It's also true that how you felt about yourself and how you carried yourself made a huge difference in how other people in your unit perceived you and that it also had an effect on your performance. Sometimes you have to have faith in yourself even when there's not a whole lot of evidence to suggest that your self-belief is founded on anything *but* faith. Doubters are going to doubt, and you have to take the mentality that you can do this thing despite what anybody else might think about your chances. I know that kind of faith in myself helped me to become a Ranger and also to achieve my goal of becoming a sniper. I had people who encouraged me, but I also know there were a lot of people questioning whether I had what it takes. If I had been one of those questioners, I wouldn't have gotten very far.

That's not to say that you shouldn't ever question yourself or that you should go around with the kind of clueless arrogance I've seen in some young guys from time to time. Quiet confidence is best, and quietly examining your doubts and fears is only natural. If you run from them, they will find you eventually, and probably at a time and place when you least want them to show up. I know it's not a part of the Special Operations mindset that many guys want to acknowledge or talk about, but in the quiet hours of the night, and not out on the battlefield, is the time to do the work you need to do to get your mind right.

I also know this: If we all had one personality trait in common, it was our desire to keep our feelings about killing bad guys to ourselves. After taking out that older Afghan man who seemed to want me to kill him, I had all kinds of mixed emotions going through me. I didn't share those with any of the guys in any detail. Even Mike, a guy I worked so closely with, wasn't someone I felt comfortable sharing my confusion with. Part of that had to do with not wanting to come across as weak. You needed guys to trust you and for them to be confident in your abilities, and vice versa. No one likes to come across as weak or less than fully competent. That was especially true with sniper/spotters. I wasn't like a lot of snipers who were what we call "kill hogs." Those kinds of guys believed that they were the ones who should be doing the vast, vast majority of the weapons firing. Their spotter was their caddy; they were the golfer. The caddy could help you out, give you numbers, but you were the only one who was going to execute the shot.

I looked at my spotter, Mike in particular, as more or less my equal. He had similar training to me and though we differed about a few things—I was never a big fan of taking a bolt-action weapon into the kind of close-range, direct-action sniping that was the bulk of the kind of combat the two of us saw together—I let him do what he thought he needed to do. He had a lot of faith in that weapon and his ability to use it, and you don't want to force a guy into doing something where he's going to feel uncomfortable and possibly be less accurate as a result. As much as we were a team, I had to recognize that there were some things he had to do his way and there were some things I had to do my way. That's what I mean about keeping track of yourself. Know what your strengths and weaknesses are and communicate them with your spotter, whether verbally or in your actions while working together.

I know that Mike and I differed in one respect: I don't think that he thought as much as me about the nature of what we did and how kills could affect us. But also, like I said, that was something we kept to ourselves, and maybe he was a better actor than I was, or maybe I wasn't able to read him as well as I could read myself. There was a lot that we shared, but still a fair amount that we kept to ourselves.

Mike and I built up a good rapport, and the bond we established is still there today. If you've read *The Reaper*, then you know that Mike and I didn't get to finish out my career together. To make a long story short, Mike got injured pretty bad when he fell down a mysterious hole. He was lucky to have survived that incident, one that is among the oddest things most of us in our unit experienced during our deployments. Since Mike was out of commission, I was assigned a new spotter.

Brent Alexander had been working out of Camp Bastion. We were both E5 sergeants, but he had two more years of service time than me. That meant that he outranked me. That he was a spotter and I was the shooter despite him being in the military longer than me wasn't unusual. Sniper teams were frequently set up like that. I never asked why that was the case, and given my attitude about how we were going to operate it seemed unimportant. One thing about Brent that did seem important to me was this: We were both nearing the end of our deployment, but Brent had yet to see any real action, and he'd recorded no kills. The guys operating out of Camp Bastion, a British base, had seen a somewhat slack period in their operational tempo.

We were working out of Camp Leatherneck, which primarily housed US Marines. Our two bases were relatively close together, so it was like Brent moved from one neighborhood in the same city to another. He was a good guy, but it was going to take some time to get used to working with somebody who was so eager to please, and pretty eager overall. I pointed out before that when you got toward the end of a deployment, you kind of eased up mentally a bit. In this case, in late summer, it wasn't so much that we were all thinking about our imminent departure, but more that we were exhausted from having gone on nearly a hundred operations in the three months we'd been in Helmand Province.

One operation seemed to blend into the next and they soon became a blur. Often during our downtime we'd sit around and shoot the shit and guys would say, "Hey, Thomas, you remember that time you walked into the side of that building?"

Thomas would look all bug-eyed and say, "What? I did what?"

He wasn't just covering for his embarrassment; he really didn't remember.

I was in the same position a bunch of times when guys hit me with the "remember when" thing and I didn't remember and said so, or pretended to go along with what they were telling me.

When Brent first reported and we met, he pressed me for details about what our element had been experiencing: "We've been hearing things, how crazy it's been for you guys. Is that true? You've all been killing guys?"

"Yeah. Dude, it's been nonstop. Every night we go out, we're under fire. We're firing."

"What weapon do you want me to bring out?"

I thought for a second. I knew that I liked to have guys make their own choices, but given what I knew about Brent—that he hadn't made any kills with a scoped weapon, that he hadn't been seeing much action—I figured he probably didn't have a preference at this point.

"Go with the SR-25. We've got to work fast."

Brent nodded, "Okay. Okay. Whatever you want me to bring out, I'll bring out. I thought maybe the Win Mag since that was what Pemberton used. Thought maybe you'd want to keep things the same."

I shrugged. "We're in a target-rich environment. I like the SR-25 for it. But it's up to you."

"No. No. I'll go with the SR." He opened his weapon case and brought the rifle out.

"Damn, that thing is clean," I said. It was; it looked like it hadn't ever been fired. "Love the paint job," I added. Brent had done it up with tiger stripes, Vietnam-era style. All of a sudden, my Dirty Diana wasn't looking as good to me.

Brent took out his scope, a Leupold Mark 6 3-18 H-58, the same one that I was using.

"We're still kicking it old school, huh?" I said.

"Minute of angle still works for me," Brent said. "I know some guys are converting to the newer Mil Relation Formula, but I believe in go with what you know."

"I hear that," I said. Brent snapped his cases shut and stowed them.

"Oh, hey," I said, trying to sound as casual as I could. "You dropped your DOPE."

A panicked look spread across Brent's face. He scanned the ground and then, as he finally got the joke, a look of anguished humor replaced his mini-terror.

"Can't believe I fell for that one," he said.

Telling a guy he'd dropped his DOPE (Data of Previous Engagements) was one of the running gags among snipers. Basically you kept your DOPE on a laminated piece of paper. Essentially it's a kind of cheat sheet or notes you keep to help you get the numbers right for a shot based on your particular weapon and technique. No two weapons fired exactly the same, so it was important to keep your DOPE.

I guess I was trying to welcome Brent to my sniper team, let him know that he was one of the guys by giving him a "remember when" kind of moment. In reality, I was happy for the guy. It sounds kind of harsh to put it this way, but doing all the training that he'd done, completing all the Sniper Schools he had, including a few I hadn't attended, and not actually getting to put those skills to use in the field must have sucked for him. Now, he was like a veteran who gets traded late in the season to a team with a chance to go to the playoffs and win it all. He's never had that opportunity before, and I don't care who you are, how stone-cold you might be, you feel happy for those kinds of guys.

Yes, he was going to go on operations where the risk level was way up there, but that's what we all played for. That was also the reason I decided that on our first operation I was going to let Brent take the lead and do the brief himself. I didn't tell him beforehand; I figured he'd been in more than enough briefs that he'd be able to handle it. So, when it was the sniper team's turn to speak up, I nudged his elbow and said, "You take it."

Again, that panicked look spread across his face— the raised eyebrows, the darting eyes, the grimace.

"No," he whispered. "You know the area better. You go."

We both stood, but I began. "So, we're going to be out there with two SR-25s. Brent will be carrying a laser rangefinder."

I went on with a long list of equipment that Brent would have with him. The guys needed to know about the laser, since its visible red dot could also be produced by an enemy's weapon. It would also be unfamiliar to our guys coming from a sniper position, because I never carried one. It was a great piece of equipment for long-range sniping, with some limitations, but for what we were doing, I didn't see the point. You had to set your rifle down or at least leave it where it was set up, get the laser, lock on a target, press the button, get the range, then go back to your weapon, make your adjustments based on that laser reading, and fire. All of that could take up precious seconds.

If you were in a hide and shooting long-range and your target wasn't on the move a lot, the thing was perfect. But we normally only had a few seconds to get our shots off. Still, if he wanted to carry it, he was welcome to use it. I liked moving light, and with all the different things that Brent was planning on taking with him—various tool kits, ammo, other supplies—I wasn't sure how he was going to be able to keep the pace we'd need. Brent was about my height, but a lot stockier, so I figured he had the heft to tote all that gear. Either that or he'd figure out pretty quickly that he'd need to rethink and adjust for the next operation. I could tell him what to do or have him learn it himself. I knew that for most guys figuring it out was better than having an answer handed to you.

It was interesting that the one thing Brent didn't carry with him was fear. And it wasn't that he was naïve and didn't understand what he was getting himself into by joining us on operations where things were likely to get hot and stay hot. In fact, as we set out that night, me sitting there with my eyes shut, Brent was messing with my radio to get back at me for the DOPE-dropping gag.

I looked at him like a mom would look at an unruly child. "Will you please? There's a time and a place for everything. Just calm down. I know you're a newbie and all, but please. Be serious, dude—we're about to go into combat."

Truth is, part of my comic response was serious—that last bit about us being about to go into combat. I know that I was feeling that little buzz of anxiety welling up in my belly. We'd taken fire, often multiple times, on seemingly every stinking one of our operations. I don't care who you are, that rubs your nerves raw. To show that, to let other guys know that you were feeling some of that, would be bad. Not just that they'd look at you funny and start to wonder, but I think we all sensed it could become contagious and multiply.

Brent and I both went to work fine-tuning our weapons and our scopes, with me fiddling with the elevation knob on my Leupold. It wasn't rotating as freely as normal, and I wondered if I had cleaned the whole apparatus as thoroughly as I could have. Out of the blue, the words of one of the commanders who'd spoken at the brief popped into my mind: "The percentages tell us that it's likely that someone is going to get shot out there." I thought about that for a minute, wondering if it was 100 percent a game of chance or if the more times I went there the greater the odds that I'd be the "one." The pilot announcing that we were ninety seconds out shut all that down.

Brent and I brought up the rear after we all unloaded. I started to call out observations and potential targets.

"Got a guy window right."

"Got a guy doorway at ten o'clock."

Almost immediately we saw tracer fire in the distance, like lightning bugs at the edge of a woods. Except those weren't trees out there, but buildings. Buildings where bad guys might be on the roof aiming down weapons at us.

I heard voices nearby, and then receding down the road as the locals alerted everybody to our presence. It was like hearing a kid making sounds into the cardboard tube of a roll of wrapping paper, and I could almost feel the vibrations up and down my body.

"Here we go, man," I said to Brent.

"You weren't kidding, were you," he responded. "This is crazy."

"Welcome to our world," I muttered as I heard the discharge of an AK coming from somewhere to my left front. "I'd be lying if I said you get used to it."

The Taliban guys were firing pop shots, a brief version of spray and pray. Just letting us know that they were out there and that they had weapons and were going to use them. Thanks. Like we hadn't figured that out by now. At this stage, unless we could identify the shooters or their locations within a few seconds, we'd just push past that point, knowing that they really weren't within effective fire range of us. We were less than three quarters of a mile into our five-mile trek to the objective, and started to pick up the pace. I looked over at Brent, and he was doing the duck-beak thing—sticking his lips out with each exhale. He was damn near carrying an entire weapons and equipment depot with him, so I wasn't surprised. What I was surprised by was how I was feeling it too.

We were on a slight rise and looking down a narrow street that led through the center of the small town. Our target for this capture-or-kill mission was an IED facilitator who was regularly spotted on the far end of the residential area. That got all our attention. IEDs were what most of us had the greatest concerns over. And as our time in country on multiple deployments lengthened, those weapons and the skill needed to utilize them had grown increasingly sophisticated. Anything we could do to end or limit their use was worth whatever we had to go through. Capturing that guy and turning him over to experts who'd question him and hopefully get the intel we needed to dismantle the whole operation was way better than getting a kill added to your tally.

We soon found ourselves in a nasty little ambush. We were taking fire from two sides, the classic "L ambush." Shots were coming at us from twelve and three o'clock. That's how it's drawn up and supposed to be done, but the guys at the three o'clock position were a little overeager. Instead of waiting for the main body of our element to draw even with their position before firing, they started shooting as soon as the lead portion, our first assault team, crossed into their view. They were firing from between buildings perpendicular to our position. That meant that they had a narrow alley to fire down. All we had to do was get to the far side of that building and hang back below the near side and their angles would be all wrong.

Since I was up toward the front, I took a knee and returned fire down that corridor, taking out a couple of them in the process. Brent was overwatching the rear portion of the element and had no shot at all. The machine gunners who were part of the first assault team also let loose, and our firepower was so superior to those bad guys at three o'clock that I figured we'd either wiped them out or they'd turned tail and run off. They must have still needed to be neutralized, because we called in Close Air Support and the A-10 Thunderbolt came in. I was amazed at how close to the ground those things flew and how maneuverable they were at low speeds. They were armed to take on tanks, and carried enough ordnance to level most of that town, but what I loved was the nose-mounted 30mm Gatling gun. The sound of that thing going off always brought a smile to my face. When the Air Force and its pilots were on scene, chances were the rest of us were going to be okay.

Brent came up to my position and we hunkered down for a few moments until the A-10 was done doing its thing. It dropped a few flares, and Brent and I squinted against the glare they produced; nighttime was turned into daytime down that short stretch of road. I took a deep breath and held it, trying to keep the smell from burning my nasal passages and throat.

"This is the real deal," Brent said.

I couldn't really tell if he was happy about that or pissed. At that point it didn't really matter. We were in the middle of it, and I knew that we weren't turning back.

Fifteen minutes after the A-10's intervention, we crossed through the town's central market area. It was a small open plaza, no more than a few hundred square yards, the size maybe of a little city playground back in Maryland where I grew up. We were somewhat vulnerable there, because surrounding the plaza were a few buildings.

"One up high!" I heard Keyes, one of the first assault team's machine gunners, shout. "One up high!"

I brought my eyes and my weapon up simultaneously, and at two o'clock there was the outline of a bad guy. He was adjusting his weapon. I could see it silhouetted as he held it out—pointing it 45 degrees away from our position. Still walking, I fired, and the man tumbled over the edge of the building landing with a heaving death sigh and the clatter of his weapon on the hard ground.

While flying in, I had already set my DOPE to three hundred yards, and that was the approximate range the guy was at. Luckiest shot of my life.

I turned and looked back at Keyes, a dude I really liked and someone who engaged in fierce trash-talking battles with me. We'd started out together in weapons squad, and our running joke was always about how cool we were. His signature line was "Dude, I'm so freakin' awesome!"

So after pulling off that shot, I had to say to him, "In case you didn't know it, I'm pretty badass."

Keyes busted out laughing, his teeth crazy white through my night vision.

"I think you need to check your underdrawers for rips, Irv, 'cause you just pulled that one out of your behind."

We bumped fists and resumed our walk through the shooting gallery of Helmand.

A few minutes after that exchange with Keyes, I heard the sound of boots coming up behind me. I glanced over my shoulder and saw Brent at my six. I slowed a bit and let him come up alongside me.

He shook his head, and a smile of appreciation washed over him. "That was some shot."

"I did not mean for that to happen," I said. "No way I could have done that if I was really trying."

"I'd take that luck any day. We all would. Luck over precision."

"Roger that," I said.

Then I heard a metallic clink sound. My first thought was "What the hell," and that was quickly followed up by an answer: Someone just threw a grenade at us!

I jumped back a bit and there was Brent bent at the waist and stooping over as if he was going to pick something up. I started thinking that, man, I'd seen that kind of stuff in World War II movies, where a GI picks up one of those German grenades that kind of looks like a little Tiki torch and then tosses it back at the Nazis. The words "potato masher" flashed through my mind, one of the nicknames for those old-time grenades. Then I started thinking how cool it was, how brave it was, how kind of crazy-ass bizarre it was that Brent was doing this movie-hero thing. All of these thoughts took up about two seconds in real time. I'd stopped walking. Brent had stopped walking. The rest of the guys kept going on toward our objective.

I saw Brent take the "grenade" and rub it up against his rifle, then hold it in place there.

"Shit. My freakin' scope fell off."

"Are you kidding me?"

"No. Can't believe it. Hope the thing isn't messed up."

Actually, I could understand how the thing fell off. I wasn't sure how his scope was affixed to his SR-25. It was either one of two ways, by quick-release tabs or by bolts. Most likely it was the quick releases. To be honest, I didn't like those older-model Leupold scopes. The optics were okay, but they were bulky and it seemed like every time you moved your weapon that scope got caught on some part of your uniform, your armor, your pack.

More and more guys from the element were passing us. We didn't have a lot of time for him to reaffix his scope.

"How the hell did it happen?" I asked, regretting it immediately, since making him answer a question was going to take away from his concentration on the task at hand.

Just as a couple of the second-team assaulters went by, I said, "Taking care of some business here. We'll be up in a minute."

Brent pulled out his tool kit and fished inside it and came up with a couple of wrenches. He started to tighten a couple of fasteners to get the scope back on. Thing was, the scope didn't just always sit in one fixed position. The weapons weren't custom-made for you, so there was some adjustability built in. You had to place your scope on the gun and then zero it—align it. Essentially that meant putting the scope in place and firing at a small target from a hundred yards away. When it was zeroed, you'd get a nice tight pattern with all five rounds. If you didn't zero your scope with your weapon, your rounds could be way off the mark.

We didn't have the time to set up for Brent to zero his weapon the right way. My mind was racing. What could we do to help him?

"We're going to have to do this the hard way," I said, "We could foresight it—"

"No need," Brent cut in. He reached into his pack and pulled out his laser rangefinder—the thing I thought was so unnecessary and clumsy to use. In this case, it was the perfect solution to a problem we shouldn't have had. Put very simply, with that laser device, he could match up what he saw through the peephole of the barrel with the crosshairs in his scope. What he'd achieve with that is what we call "combat zero." Not as precise as you'd like as a sniper, but you'd still be able to get very, very close, if not directly on target. You might not be able to shoot the fly on a guy's nose, but you'd definitely be able to hit the guy.

With his scope reattached, I said to him, "Let's roll."

"Sorry about that," Brent said.

"No worries," I told him. "But you do know that this time you really did drop your DOPE."

"Funny," he grunted. "You shouldn't be enjoying my pain this much."

I wasn't enjoying it at all, but I wanted him to loosen up a bit. While we'd been working on an aiming solution and he was reattaching his scope, Brent was beating himself up pretty bad for his mistake. I knew about being hard on yourself, and I thought a little joke and not a pep talk was what he needed.

I was worried about letting the guys know that we were down one sniper. They didn't need to have that in the back of their minds. I flashed back to the time that Mike's weapon had completely failed to fire and how chaotic all of that was. Didn't need a repeat, and I trusted that Brent would be good to go even without the best targeting system.

At least we could count on one thing: About every three quarters of a mile we ran into more enemy fire. Mostly, Brent and I were able to hang back a bit. The line guys took care of things, so it was hustle, shoot, hustle most of the way to the objective. Brent and I both fired a few times, but the resistance we encountered was fairly light, though still very irritating.

Once we arrived at the objective, it was the usual thing—climb on a roof to do our overwatch. The only thing different about this night was that we were working with what most of us called the Afghan Army, or the ANA. Officially they were members of the Afghan National Army, the main branch of the Afghan Armed Forces. At first, I wasn't cool with the idea of fighting alongside those guys, but I was getting more used to the idea. My experience with them took place before any of the incidents in which Afghan Army guys turned on other members of their units or other coalition forces. Mostly I didn't like them criticizing us during debriefs and telling us how we were doing things wrong or were being too rough on people. "It's a war!" I kept wanting to shout at them.

That night, the Afghans and our assault teams went into the building together. We also had a couple of interpreters with us, and I felt bad for those guys and what happened to some of them. The Taliban considered the interpreters traitors and went after them, and more often their families. Sometimes the Taliban turned those interpreters against us. I don't know what I would have done if I was in their shoes—having my family threatened unless I did what they told me to do. While I was overwatching and thinking about those other things, Brent was working on trying to get a quick foresight with his weapon. That involved some disassembly, and he had his weapon in pieces. As it turned out, things at the objective and with our HVT were going better than our approach had.

I could tell from seeing bad guys being led away from the house with their hands zip-tied behind them that we were close to wrapping things up. I told Brent that he didn't have much time.

"Shit. Shit. Shit," he mumbled. He sat there with the bulk carrier in his hands and looked up at me. "Why am I such a shithead? I suck. I'm not going to get this thing together in time."

"Don't worry about it. I got things under control. We're fine. I had to do this a few times myself before you got here, so it's not like it's sucking too bad right now."

He didn't want to hear that.

"I let you down, man."

He sounded really depressed. I figured I'd do what we always did with one another when a guy was feeling down—give him more shit. "When I found out it was you who was coming in to replace Mike, I kind of figured there'd be a bunch of fuckups, so I was prepared for all of this nonsense."

Brent's grunt laugh let me know I'd done the right thing. Next, I heard the call that the element would be moving. I relayed that message to Brent and added, "I'm going to face out." I turned to six o'clock so that I was facing the same direction as the rest of the guys as we headed back. I traced the path of our extraction route, looking for anything suspicious. We only had to go a little less than a mile, but with all the delays we'd had because of the short firefights on the way in, the sky was starting to lighten. As the other guys moved out, I refreshed my ammo, swapping a partially spent magazine for a full one and making sure that another full one was at the ready on my belt rig.

It seemed as if the approaching sunrise roused a bunch of locals. They started coming out of their houses, a number of them pointing, which got me on high alert. I hated pointers, because I had to think that they were spotters for the Taliban. I immediately got on the comms and let my main element leader know that there was a lot of movement among the locals. I got that feeling in my stomach that it was about to be game time.

"You good to go?" I asked Brent.

"I think so. I think I'll be on target."

"Well, we're going to find out real soon, I think."

His weapon was back together, but he hadn't been able to use the foresight technique to get his weapon and sighting properly calibrated.

Despite that, I said to him, "Dude, you've got all the targets from here on out."

Whatever beating up he'd done to himself didn't leave any marks. Brent didn't smile, but his tone was a whole light lighter and sharper than it had been when he was dumb-assing himself.

We joined the guys on a road that ran alongside a clear running stream. Morning mist rose off the water. In the distance ground fog shrouded the scrub grass and the stunted trunks of trees rose out of it like the legs of cartoon sheep. The hairs on the back of my neck stood up. This was not good.

I looked through my scope, and with the sun so low on the horizon, the fog, the mist, the monochrome landscape, everything was indistinct. Ahead of us was a larger village than the one we'd just been in, and between us and it ran a long flat cultivated field, dark furrows icing the top layer of soil. A little shy of a mile away, a man stood in that field, far, too far really, from any kind of building to have just woken up and stepped out to go to work. I detected movement, and squinted harder against the lens of my scope, wishing that the light was better. I thought that maybe he was shrugging his way into a chest rack—a tactical vest that holds ammunition and is held up by suspenders. The only reason you put one of those on is if you're planning on doing some shooting.

Given the lighting conditions and the ground fog, for all we knew dozens and dozens of bad guys could have been in that field.

I radioed what I'd spotted to Captain Arnold.

"Can you reach him?"

"Negative. Not from this elevation." The ammo I had with me wasn't designed to carry that distance, and with only a 10x power scope my sighting wouldn't be good enough either. The best that round could do was maybe six tenths of a mile. For a second I thought of Mike and his Win Mag, and that maybe I should have told Brent to carry his. I didn't linger on that too long. Second-guessing wasn't going to do us any good.

I was in the middle of an exchange with Captain Arnold about how I needed to get up high to even consider taking a shot at that figure out on the farm when I heard the *tink-tink, tink-tink* sound of an AK being discharged. The sound was coming from behind us, from the small village we'd just left that was now at our six o'clock position. A bunch of locals were all standing there looking out at us. None of them were moving much, and it was pretty clear that none of them were doing the firing. Rounds started to come in pretty hot at that point, but we couldn't return fire. If we took out any of those unarmed watchers, there'd be hell to pay and then some. We had no choice but to drop down and try to take cover as best we could.

The snipers got the call to get into position. We're the only ones who can do the kind of precise shooting neces-sary to take out a bad guy with a weapon who's moving in and among a group of unarmed locals providing him with cover. I scope out a guy with an AK. He's hunched over. Picture a chessboard after a dozen or so turns. You've got people spread out a bit, pawns and rooks and knights and bishops. In the back row, the queen is hunkered down, using as many of those other pieces as possible cover. There's alleys and lanes between them all; they haven't formed a solid wall. I can fire through those lanes. But I have to be dead-on with those shots; otherwise, there will be someone I shouldn't have shot dead on that board.

We'd done drills like this in training and it was one of the toughest mind games I'd ever played, a brain-busting, nerve-twanging kind of mind fuck that is a mash-up of calculations and doubts and hopes. What I'd figured out was that I had to toss all of that out of my mind and get back to the most basic kind of targeting. Pick one small thing on that target, eliminate everything else in that scope's magnified circle, and do what you've trained your body to do. Step aside, brain, I got this one.

I fired the first round at the AK man, and missed just short of him. A few of the other rooks and knights heard the round go by an adjacent square, and they twitched. A second round was a bit closer, but it got the other pieces to scatter. The third one took out the AK queen in the back row. All the rest of the chess pieces scattered at this point, running off the board and into the box, figuring that their little tactic had failed big-time, thinking, "Those guys out there, those Americans, have some kind of skill, and though we figured we'd be safe knowing they wouldn't take out an unarmed guy, we didn't figure they'd do this." They weren't thinking enough moves in advance.

Brent and I were still lying prone and scanning when a guy came flying around a corner of one of the village's squat little huts. He was tearing across the little bit of open ground and the embankment that led down to the stream. He was heading toward a point where some tall grass and reeds stuck up out of the water and would have afforded him a bit of a hide. A few of the line guys fired their M4s at him. I counted seven shots.

"DrophimDrophimDrophim," I said to Brent, not shouting but running the words all together as quick as I could.

His weapon clicked off safety. "Watch me. Watch me. Keep track," Brent said, more calmly than I would have thought possible under the circumstances.

I was ready to spot for him, and when his first round left the barrel I tried to track it. It was so far off target I knew he had to make some major adjustments. "Four mils left. You need to come down six." Figures and calculations were flashing through my mind as I watched the guy scramble down that slope and then stop. He must have thought better of his choice, and now he was hightailing it back toward the village. I gave Brent another set of instructions and heard him making all the corrections on his adjusters and knobs. He zeroed out that rifle faster than anyone I'd ever seen.

He fired, and dust clouds kicked up at the bad guy's left foot.

"Another half mil up and you've got him."

Brent adjusted and got the guy dead center in the back. The man somersaulted and then lay flat near the entrance to a narrow alley. Another twenty steps and he'd have made it. Too bad for him.

"Got him. Got him," Brent said, and then added, "My rifle's zeroed. I'm good to go now."

"Let's target."

At that point, we got intel from our line guys that back in the field behind us, more bad guys were springing up.

"RPGs. RPGs. AKs," Long, one of the weapons team guys, reported. "One o'clock. One-thirty. Three hundred fifty yards."

I was scoping that area and saw the bad guy, but no way that was three hundred fifty yards. I dialed in for five hundred.

"Brent. I'm getting like five hundred yards."

I have to admit that I didn't think this at the time, but after Brent and I talked about it. With how quickly things were going down, there was no way that laser range-finder would have done us any good. I'm not antitech-nology now and I wasn't then, but you need the right tool for the right job, and that tool wasn't it. In fact, after that first operation with me, Brent stowed that thing away and it never saw action after that.

We'd both scrambled to the ground again at that point. I had a rock digging into my pelvis. I used another rock to help support my elbow. One leg of my bipod was extended to the ground, the other was hanging free. Not exactly ideal shooting range conditions, but that was Afghanistan. I could then see that at least three others had joined the first guy Long had radioed to us about, more or less evenly spaced a few yards apart in a kind of V formation.

"Take him," I said to Brent.

He fired and missed the first guy by inches.

"Come three mils right."

A second passed, and then I heard a boom and watched as the guy toppled to the ground.

That set the other three guys in motion, moving left to right across my field of vision. The terrain was more rolling than I realized at first, and he made it down a shallow incline. He kept going, heading for a rock outcropping. But he had a ways to go, so I was able to track him and bring him down.

What happened next is frozen in my memory. I don't know a whole lot about optics and the nature of light, but as murky and dim as things seemed when this firefight started, when I went to scope out the next guy, the conditions had changed a ton. Later on, somebody told me about the golden hour, the time that photographers love early in the morning. There's a clarity to the air that makes pictures so pure and clean. As I looked through the scope, I must have experienced that phenomenon. Usually I was firing at night, so I never got to experience this, but now something clicked in my brain and whatever else I was thinking and feeling was replaced by a kind of serenity and pleasure that you would never expect to feel under these circumstances.

I aimed and let loose with another round, and as it left the barrel, I could follow its path and saw as the bullet rotated and wobbled slightly. It was only slightly off mark and I told myself, "Hold up two and right one." The bullet came out and hit the apex. Even before it reached the guy, I knew it was right on target.

"That's tracking," I said under my breath. I'd held right one because of the wind, and I watched that breeze nudge the round back left and it was like I'd thrown this very long and very fast curveball and it drifted right into the strike zone, right into where the catcher was holding his glove. It drifted left a bit more and took the guy out.

I'd just fired the longest shot I'd ever taken at a human being, and it had been a good one. It was just over a half mile. Not bad for a direct-action sniper who had taken out most of his targets from between a hundred and three hundred yards.

Funny enough, the rest of that operation is kind of a blur to me. I know that the firefight didn't last much longer. I do remember standing overwatch for the guys while they did their ID of the dead bad guys. By that time, the light wasn't golden any longer, but I stood on a small rise surveying the scene. It was like I could see forever out to the curved horizon. I was really happy for Brent. He'd popped his sniper cherry. He'd messed up a bit with dropping his scope, but seeing how he responded and got his act back together and zeroed out that weapon when we really needed him to made me feel pretty damn good. I know he felt the same way, and that was the start of a brief, but very productive partnership. He dropped his DOPE, but things picked up from there.

I didn't think it was possible, but we ended up having a good night in Helmand after a really, really bad night. Even the chow tasted better when we got back behind the wire. I wasn't about to suggest to Brent what he should eat. Like a lot of things out there, that was something he would be better off figuring out for himself. I was just going to take care of myself, and trust that Brent would figure it all out.

EIGHT

TIMING IS EVERYTHING

AT THE TAIL end of the summer of 2009, when I'd had the fortunate good streak that resulted in me making thirty-three kills and earning the nickname "The Reaper," our whole unit was feeling pretty good about ourselves. Not only had I set that record, but we'd discovered and destroyed a bunch of weapons caches, dismantled a number of weapons-making operations, and limited the Taliban's economic capability by interfering with their heroin sales. Our operational tempo had been off the charts. It was go, go, go, and in a lot of ways that was good. As humans we crave consistency, and most people operate at their best when they can get into a rhythm.

That's really true of being a sniper as well. When you're out on the range or shooting in a competition, you find your tempo and stick with it. You get on a roll and settle into a groove, which can really help you. Rush too much and you make an error and miss a target; then you have to fight the urge to speed up. You want to make up for the mistake, but by being too focused on speed and getting to the next target, you're just going to get yourself into more trouble.

A lot of other guys in other units suffered from the hurry-up-and-waits. You go downrange, you hustle to get settled in, and then it's like someone puts the brakes on. You don't go out on an operation for a few days, you lose a bit of your battle-readiness, you have too much time on your hands and start to think a little too much about what's going on back home, what's going on outside the wire, too much about what dangers you might face. When you finally get the call, it's rushrushrush. Then you face another lull of a few days, sometimes a few weeks, and you lose your edge again. Those are tough circumstances to deal with. Time and timing have to be your friends; and like you sometimes have to do with your friends, you have to make accommodations. Time won't always be on your side, so you have to adjust. Knowing how to work with time is a key element to success in anything, including sniping and facing any enemy contact.

Fortunately for us during the period when I earned

the nickname "The Reaper," we had that high tempo throughout. And as the last days of our deployment approached, the tempo was still high, but the commanders let up on us a little bit during our downtime.

One afternoon in late July of 2009, I was walking down the hallway of our quarters, and in each room I passed I heard something unusual—the sound of music. Normally we could listen to it with our headphones on, but that was it. Our CO Captain Arnold didn't officially make an announcement that we could play it out loud, but when our platoon sergeant, Mack, didn't come and tell us to shut it down, we figured we were good to go with our impromptu Afghan summer concert.

Walking down that hallway, it was like listening to the end-of-year Top 100 countdown. Gnarls Barkley's "Crazy" was mixing it up with Ne-Yo's "So Sick." I suddenly felt a bit queasy when Dominick Fratelli, one of the weapons squad guys from the Bronx, came out of his room in nothing but his boxers and his Yankees hat lip-synching to Shakira's "Hips Don't Lie." He was using a hairbrush as a microphone, and with the other hand he was wagging his finger at me and then signaling that he wanted me to follow him into his room.

I did what he asked, and there, spread out on his bed, was an American flag.

"You gotta sign this," he said over the music. "Make sure you put 'Reaper' and '33.'"

I leaned over and, with a Sharpie, did as he asked.

"Going down in history, baby!" he shouted as I walked out of his room laughing.

I joined a bunch of the other guys and it was as close to a party atmosphere as we could have out there. I remembered watching *M*A*S*H*, and I wished that we had something like the bar where those doctors used to hang out. The COs had loosened up a bit on us, but they weren't going to tolerate any kind of alcohol consumption. We had to be ready to go out on a moment's notice.

Since we were heading back home in a few hours, guys relaxed on the hoarding of favorites they'd gotten in their care packages from loved ones.

Some of the Hispanic guys got the best of that deal. They set out some of the "candy" that they'd been sent. I'll never forget the look on Wagner's face when he tore open the wrapper of an innocent-looking piece of hard candy, put it in his mouth, sucked on it for a few seconds, and then spit it out. He was gagging and stomping his feet before downing a Gatorade in record time.

"What the hell, bro? Candy's supposed to be sweet. That shit is HOT!" he finally managed to say as we all rolled around laughing at his red-faced pain.

"You got to maintain your situational awareness," Martinez said. "Don't you read labels, dude?"

He bent over and retrieved the paper that Wagner's candy had been wrapped in. He held it up for all of us to see.

"Pulparindo," he said slowly, like my high school Spanish teacher used to.

"That don't mean shit to me," Wagner said, tears running down his cheeks.

"It don't have to," Johnson said, taking the wrapper from Martinez and showing it to the rest of us. "Look at the cartoon dude on there."

Sure enough, the little red figure—I couldn't tell whether he was an animal or a vegetable—had fire streaming out of his mouth.

"Damn," Wagner said, clearly enjoying being the center of attention. "Give a boy a warning next time. Tissue damage going on in here," he said, sticking out his tongue.

The sound of our pagers going off ended the party. We all looked at our devices and then rushed for the door.

Time-sensitive target.

We had minutes to get ready and into the briefing room. As relaxed and casual as we'd been just moments before, we were now all in high gear.

As I ran toward my room, I took a quick stop in Brent's. He wouldn't be joining us on this one, but I wanted to make sure I took the time to see him. He was heading home, what we called "ripping out," so that meant I wouldn't see him before we left.

"I got to go plan this op," I said. I held out my hand. "I'll see you when I get back to Benning."

"Good luck, man. Be safe."

"That's the plan."

I dashed off to the mission room for the briefing. We were advised that not only was this a time-sensitive target, meaning that we had just a few minutes to get ready before insertion, but that this high-value target had been eluding us for months. He was one of the chief leaders of a large Taliban unit. It almost seemed like he had a mole working for him on the inside. Every time we'd gone after him, with good intel from reliable sources letting us know of his location, he'd somehow slipped away. Even before we'd arrived, another Ranger squad had tried to track him down, with no luck. We wanted this bad guy in the worst way. So it was going to be out the door and wheels up ASAP.

I edged my way through a hallway crowded with guys throwing on clothes and grabbing gear to get to the ready room. I spotted Wayne, the weapons team guy who'd been assigned to me. I was going out as the lone sniper on this op. I didn't have much time, but I wanted to be sure to at least check in with Wayne and let him know directly—outside the context of the briefing room, where you could get overwhelmed by all the information—what our specific role was going to be. Yes, time was at a premium, but as is true of all aspects of being a sniper, you have to know how to use time to your advantage. We were all hurrying, but if he didn't understand his roles and responsibilities going in, there wouldn't be

A team photo taken near the end of our 90-day deployment in and around Tikrit, Iraq, in 2006. We conducted more than 120 operations during that period.

THE UNITED STATES OF AMERICA

TO ALL WHO SHALL SEE THESE PRESENTS, GREETING:

THIS IS TO CERTIFY THAT
THE SECRETARY OF DEFENSE
HAS AWARDED

THE JOINT SERVICE ACHIEVEMENT MEDAL

TO

PRIVATE FIRST CLASS NICHOLAS G. IRVING, UNITED STATES ARMY

FOR
MERITORIOUS SERVICE
FOR THE ARMED FORCES OF THE UNITED STATES
FROM ___ 2006 TO ___ 2006
GIVEN UNDER MY HAND THIS 18TH DAY OF JULY, 2006

JOINT TASK FORCE
COMMAND OR OFFICE

STANLEY A. McCHRYSTAL, LTG, USA, COMMANDING
SECRETARY OF DEFENSE

DD FORM 2414, MAY 1999

The certificate that accompanied the Joint Service Award medal I received as a young machine gunner. I assisted other members of our team in securing a downed little bird, an MH-6 attack helicopter.

Another Ranger and I at the International Sniper Competition in 2009, using the lessons we learned from urban combat operations. We managed to crack the top five.

The official platoon photo from my first Afghanistan deployment, taken shortly before we departed Kandahar Airport.

Posing in 2008 on a rooftop in Afghanistan. This was my first deployment as a designated marksman and using a precision rifle.

Out in the field during one of my first training exercises before deploying to Iraq as a young machine gunner.

U.S.-led forces kill 15 alleged terrorists

BY SAMEER N. YACOUB
The Associated Press

BAGHDAD — U.S.-led forces killed 15 terror suspects and detained three others during raids Tuesday in a village northeast of Baghdad, the military said. Residents said 13 civilians also were killed.

Elsewhere, a bombing killed four people in a Baghdad market and a suicide bomber blew himself up in a home for the elderly in the southern city of Basra, killing two.

Also, from London, a senior British commander said Tuesday that the security situation is worsening in Basra, Iraq's second largest city, as coalition forces prepare to hand over security responsibilities to nearby areas to Iraqi troops.

Lt. Gen. Nick Houghton also told Britain's House of Commons that a power struggle among Shiite factions in Basra, and attacks by their militias, have led to increased violence in the southern city, which was once thought to be one of Iraq's most receptive areas to the U.S.-led invasion.

The U.S. military said the raid targeted individuals linked with a suspected senior

Victims arrive at a hospital in Baqouba, after U.S.-led forces killed 15 terror suspects and detained three others. A fierce gunfight broke out during simultaneous raids targeting a senior al-Qaida member, according to the U.S. military, in the village of Bushahin north of Baqouba on Tuesday

ADAM HADI

nine armed terrorists on the rooftop," the U.S. military said in a statement. It said five militants v   ied by coalition air-

ty because he feared retribution, confirmed the civilian deaths, saying 12-year-old boy was among them.

A news report from our mission (what I came to call the Chicken Coop) in Iraq. Rarely did any of the work we did make the news.

During the International Sniper Comp, going over a game plan on what DOPE to use to engage movers at 700 meters. No misses this event, despite not using Dirty Diana, my SR-25.

CITATION

TO ACCOMPANY THE AWARD OF

THE JOINT SERVICE ACHIEVEMENT MEDAL

TO

PRIVATE FIRST CLASS NICHOLAS G. IRVING

UNITED STATES ARMY

Private First Class Nicholas G. Irving, United States Army, distinguished himself by exceptionally meritorious achievement as a Machine Gunner for a Joint Task Force in support of Operation IRAQI FREEDOM from 20 June 2006 to 21 June 2006. During this period, Private First Class Irving demonstrated outstanding determination while involved in combat missions. Receiving heavy enemy fire, he provided cover for the main assault on the objective and demonstrated great effort in securing a downed aircraft and the crew. The distinctive accomplishments of Private First Class Irving reflect credit upon him, the United States Army, and the Department of Defense.

The citation accompanying my Joint Service Award.

(Above) Pemberton looks on as I do some pistol training with one of our nation's elite allies a couple of weeks prior to heading off to Afghanistan in 2009.

(Left) Sitting on the airfield about to conduct the last jump of my career. The look on my face says it all. I hate jumping out of aircraft.

Running out of the back of a Stryker with one of my spotters during another sniper competition.

One of my brothers in arms carrying a wounded member of our team—a military working dog—to an extraction point. That dog had saved a bunch of lives that day.

On our way to conduct a TST operation in Helmand Province.

Performing during an urban combat training exercise a few weeks prior to deploying to Afghanistan.

My going-away plaque draped with the same shemagh I wore while deployed.

Dirty Diana!

Graduation day in 2007. During Ranger school I shed more than 30 pounds. Soon after, I would deploy to Iraq as a designated marksman and machine gun team leader.

time for questions and answers later on, when we had enemy contact; it would be time for action.

"Your job is just to be at my six. I'll be on overwatch. There's a cluster of eight buildings in that compound. My plan is to be on top of one of them at about nine o'clock to the objective. There's nothing behind that building as far as I can tell. You'll be scanning that area."

"Got it," Wayne said. "I'll be there."

I looked around the ready room at the thirty other guys putting the finishing touches on their kit.

"We all will," I said to Wayne, nodding toward them. "We've got them. You've got me. Everything's good."

I had Wayne sit next to me during the briefing in case he had any questions; I didn't want to take up everybody's time with them if it wasn't necessary. As it turned out, Wayne was good to go without any additional elaboration from me or the other team leaders.

As soon as we were on the tarmac of the airfield, mortar rounds came in on our position. I thought again about our HVT and what seemed to be his sixth sense. As I hustled aboard the Chinook, I wondered if maybe somebody was tipping him off—one of the Afghan interpreters? Some other local who worked with us or for us? Seemed too coincidental that as soon as we were off to get a bad guy, explosive rain came down near us.

In keeping with our time-sensitive mission, the chopper pilots did their part to deliver us to the landing zone as quick as possible. As much as I have a fear of heights,

I liked it when the pilots employed their map-the-earth routine. That meant low-altitude flying, adjusting the craft's flight for terrain and man-made obstacles. At other points in the quick flight to the LZ, we climbed steeply. A bit of a roller-coaster ride, but varying our altitude was just another way to keep safe.

As soon as the skids hit the ground, we were sprinting off that bird. We didn't take any time to do any real observation/reconnaissance. The compound was in the middle of a clearing. Trees framed the clearing. Half our team had been dropped off on the far side of the objective, approaching from east to west. We were running through a freshly tilled farm field. The dirt was soft and furrows staggered us and made the going especially tough. I tried to take my mind off my burning thighs and hamstrings by visualizing what it must have looked like for us to come in low and fast, burst out of the chopper, and take off like we were a bunch of Delta guys. Should have used us for a recruitment video.

As we got within a few hundred yards of the objective, I was able to make out some of the features I'd seen back in our brief. I started counting the small buildings dotting the compound, orienting myself to their positions relative to the objective and to one another. It was clear that this wasn't organized like the orderly subdivisions back home, with each house aligned with every other one, all of them with their entrances perpendicular to gridlike streets. Instead, it looked as if the wind had blown and scattered them across this high-desert land-scape.

The buildings were clustered in a loose circle, like a cog gear with a few teeth missing. I spotted the one at roughly nine o'clock that I'd identified as the best posi-tion for Wayne and me. I started angling toward it. The ground beneath our feet had gone from tilled soil to hardpan; now we were on to loose stones ("baby heads," some guys called them), rocks the approximate size of a newborn's skull. They led down to an irrigation ditch. I was slip-sliding along them, cursing under my breath, but when I looked to either side of me, I didn't see any rocks at all. What the hell?

My geological contemplation was cut short by the sound of tracers overhead. Good thing I'd gone down that incline and wasn't any taller. I threw myself against the far side of the ditch and hunkered down. We were taking fire, and because we were so near to being sent home, and it was so soon after one of our guys, Benjamin Kopp, had been killed in action, I was really, really in no mood for being shot at. Screw the whole acting-like-a-superhero thing I had once done. I was staying down until there was a lull in the firing. Time was slipping away, but what good would it do to get myself shot and impact the operation by having to have guys come in to help me? There's a time for everything, I reminded myself.

When the first lull came, I jumped up and quickly

fired a few rounds without aiming. I also took that opportunity to survey the scene. Ahead of me our assaulters weren't taking their time like I had been. They were advancing, taking a knee to fire, advancing. We had to be there in support of them, so I motioned to Wayne (who was doing the right thing by hanging back behind me) that we had to join them. It was like we were all engaged in a game of leapfrog. Run. Crouch. Run. Crouch.

Even before I reached the sniper perch I'd decided on, I heard the sound of the flash bombs and other concussive and explosive devices.

"Shit," I thought, "the other teams are starting. We should have been up on a roof doing our job."

I had to make a quick call.

"Up here. Now," I said to Wayne.

He turned to me, and I unsnapped the ladder and leaned it up against the wall. Instead of being at the nine o'clock, we were somewhere between six and seven. As soon as I had a moment, I got on the radio to alert the team leaders and everyone else on the main radio frequency of the change in my location. I wanted all the friendlies to know where Wayne and I were. On some operations, I lived in fear that some guy's comms would be down and he wouldn't get the message, then he'd see a figure up on a roof with a weapon and decide to take a shot at me.

I started up the ladder, and when I got to the top I extended my left hand beyond the ledge, expecting to reach the roof; instead, I reached nothing but air. I clambered back down and said to Wayne, "There's no roof. We've got to get up somewhere. Now."

We each grabbed an end of the ladder and took off running. As much as I hated that there was no roof there, I took a moment to survey the scene as we ran. We were losing time, but at least we were gaining intelligence. I detected movement to my left, in the trees, just north of where we'd come in through that plowed field. I knew that this situation was about to get bad, but at least I knew it. I got on the radio and reported what I'd seen. The assaulters were busy, occupied with going from building to building. I could hear them doing their thing—breaching the doors with C-4, popping flash bombs, yelling. Our target must not have been in the first three buildings I heard being cleared. But I needed to see our guys at work and not just hear them.

Wayne and I pulled up at the original building I had ID'd as my position. I went back on the radio to alert everybody. I came up with a game plan on the fly and shared it with Wayne. We were three hundred yards from the tree line and half that distance from the house that was the original objective. That objective was surrounded by a waist-high wall. Wayne joined me on the roof.

"I may be moving around some, but you've got to keep your eye on that ladder. Make sure nobody takes it."

I'd heard of the bad guys doing that a few times and

I didn't want to be stranded up there, or have to jump down, or have to climb off that roof and really expose myself to the enemy.

"If we start to take fire from below, from inside this house, you get the hell off this roof instantly."

Along with my fear of friendly fire was another fear. If we were on top of the bad guys and they heard us up here, what was to keep them from firing through the mud roof to take us out? If that kind of fire started, I'd be able to get to the ledge, where the wall met the roof, and have a better chance of not getting hit. Even better, instead of tactical boots, which would have offered good protection but were loud, I always wore soft-soled shoes. I tiptoed all around those rooftops like a stealthy cat.

We took up our positions and watched the assaulters do their thing. Even though we were really in a hurry and these guys were moving fast, it wasn't like they were rushing at all. I've heard athletes say that in the middle of all the action in a game, they see things as moving slowly. I experienced that a lot overseas when we were in contact with the enemy. The action seemed to slow down, but time was still moving normally. I watched the assaulter move in, take off his backpack device, stick it to the door frame, and then look overhead at me. He gave me the thumbs-up and I returned it.

"Roger that, I got you," I heard him say over the comms. "You might want to hunker down for this one. It's a big one."

I did as I'd observed them do: I prepared to eat the blast. That's what they called it when you opened your mouth and shut your eyes. Somehow by opening your mouth you made the pressure inside your head more equal to the concussion wave of the explosion. I pressed myself as flat as I could, did a three count, and then ate the blast. The roof vibrated and wavered a bit before settling back into position. I stood and scoped the doors and windows, scanned up and down the sides of the house, making sure no squirters came out. I spotted two guys running, weaving in and out around some things I couldn't quite make out. I could see that they were unarmed. I couldn't take them out, but I wanted to keep them from leaving the area. I fired a few shots just ahead of each of them as they tore off for the trees. I don't know if they didn't see the dust kicked up in front of them or didn't hear the round, but once they took off in that sprint for the woods, nothing was going to stop them.

When the AC-130's spotlight settled into place, I got a better view of them. They were definitely unarmed, a couple of young guys—military-aged males: MAMs— as oblivious to the infrared light tracking them as they were to me firing at them. Over the comms I heard the report of three MAMs fleeing. I didn't see the third guy, but presumed that he'd split off from the other two before I'd spotted. A small team from our element was going to go bring them in.

I was instructed to concentrate on my overwatch of

the assault teams' attempt to locate our chief bad guy. With two teams working simultaneously on different buildings, it was like watching two chess games going on at the same time as our guys moved around the compound. To my far left, I saw our ground force commander (GFC) and radio operator on the edge of the compound, coordinating things among the teams, the eyes in the sky, and back behind the wire.

"We've got movement! We've got movement!" Wayne hissed at me. I pivoted and swung my rifle around to scan Wayne's area. At least four figures were moving toward us, coming in from the same direction we'd taken, through the same plowed field.

"You've got possible enemy packs coming, closing in to our position," I radioed.

The ground force commander looked up at me and shook his head, acknowledging that he'd received the message I'd sent over the comms. He also was indicating that he felt the same way as we all did about that deployment in Afghanistan. It seemed like whenever we were out there operating, things could be going along fairly smoothly and to plan, when suddenly more of these fighters came out of the woodwork like roaches. That sounds kind of harsh and it is intended to be, since these guys were always making our lives more difficult and were trying to *take* our lives. What it doesn't reveal is the grudging respect they earned. Even me calling them "fighters" says something about that.

These guys were better trained, more disciplined, and more courageous than the bad guys we'd faced in Iraq. I'm not the greatest student of history, but I knew that these people had fought off the Russian army. Maybe not these guys specifically, but their fathers and uncles and elders. It's not like I was thinking that we should be handing out medals to these guys, because I also knew that the Taliban did some nasty things to their own people, as well as to us. Respect meant acknowledging that they could do us harm—that we shouldn't overlook their capability and let our guard down.

The ground force commander, GFC Duns, went up the chain of command with this new intel. A few moments later he reported back to me that we were okay to take these guys out if we determined that they posed a threat to the assaulters or to me. On the one hand, I felt good that the guys in command trusted my judgment. On the other hand, I also knew that if some investigator later on reviewed the kill and ruled against my judgment, I could end up in prison. That's a lot to have going through your mind. What made it particularly difficult was that it was clear that a few of these guys were armed. Some of them weren't, though. Or at least I hadn't been able to confirm their status. I encountered that a few times in Afghanistan, and it always messed with my mind.

Just because you were with a group of guys who were armed, did that mean you deserved to be shot and killed?

It's easy to make an assumption in theory and say, "Hell, yes, they should be fair game." But a lot of times, as I wrote before, people were milling around in the town and they may or may not have been offering aid and assistance to the armed bad guys. When you got the responsibility placed on your shoulders, it also meant that the consequences were on you. You really had to think about what you were doing and why. Thinking took time, and you didn't want to do anything that might jeopardize the safety of your own men. I would never do anything to increase the chances of us losing a guy, but I also had to factor in if this was a legitimate kill. As you can tell, it was easy to have your thoughts get all jumbled up.

When I saw more movement within the tree line, I decided it was time to end the debate and to go into action. I eased my weapon off safety and got myself into the best possible firing position. I lay prone, with the bipod set up just a few inches this side of the edge of the roof.

"Wayne, I need you to help me split these targets," I said. I could only focus on one sector, and on who populated that sector, at a time. He'd have to fill in for me in performing the overwatch on our guys within the compound. At six hundred–plus yards, the "invaders" were outside of Wayne's M4 range. I took the time to formulate the first of my miniplans. I'd work from left to right. At the extreme, one of the armed guys would be coming within better range and almost straight on to my position. I'd take him out and then move to the left and the next target. He was quite a bit ahead of the first guy, by more than fifty yards.

They were smart. By their not staying at the same distance from my position, I'd have to take the time to do more calculations and retargeting. That was critical, because in that gap between my being able to send rounds on those two different targets, the second guy, and the third and fourth and who-knew-how-many other bad guys out there, could be on the move—either moving away from us or, as they'd shown the tendency to do, or moving closer to us, posing more of a threat to overrun our position.

"I'm going to send one," I said to Wayne.

"Which target first?" he asked.

"Far left."

"Got it. I can see him." By "see" I knew that what Wayne meant he could spot was little more than a bright blob in his night vision goggles. As a member of the assault team, he wasn't fitted with night vision goggles that had the proper magnification for him to see long distances.

"Get your light on that target for me," I instructed. I was taking deep breaths, trying to clear any kind of nervous energy from my muscles and my mind. I shut everything else out of my mind and my field of vision except for that figure in my scope. I let out the slack on the trigger and prepared myself for the discharge down-range.

I squeezed the trigger the rest of they way, and instead of the familiar hard *crump* sound I normally heard, I heard a kind of *pffft thunk*. An instant later I felt something prickling my cheeks, something warm and sharp, uncomfortable but not terribly painful. Immediately my mind was racing, trying to determine what had happened. With my eye still pressed to the scope, I could see a smoky fog rising up. Still feeling a bit stunned, I wondered if maybe one of our guys or maybe theirs had popped smoke. But why?

The smoke cleared and I looked down at Duns, the ground commander, and he was looking up at me.

"Sniper One, are you okay?"

"Fine," I said. "Just not sure what the hell happened."

"Did you take a round on your position? Are you hit?"

"I don't think so."

"Saw an impact just in front of your position."

I didn't respond. I still wasn't sure what was going on, but I did see that the first target I'd selected was moving forward. He took a position within the irrigation ditch, just like I had, pressing himself tight against the embankment nearest to me. I had a little more than a torso in my line of sight, a much smaller target than before.

I took my time and re-aimed. I squeezed the trigger

and the same thing happened as before. My eye stung this time, as if somebody had tossed sand in it. With each blink, a bit of the grit scraped my eyeball.

"Son of a bitch," I thought. "What is happening?"

"Weapon malfunction?" Wayne asked.

I pulled my head back and away from the scope. I sighted along the barrel and immediately shut my eyes and shook my head in disgust. So much for really taking my time and being certain everything was squared away. The scope, obviously, sits on top of the barrel. When I sighted through it, I had a perfectly clear line of vision on the target. I thought I was good to go and had accounted for the raised lip of the edge of the roof.

I hadn't.

I'd fired two rounds directly into that lip, kicking up stones and dirt.

Total rookie mistake to not factor in the mechanical offset in the equations I'd been doing. On an AR-15, the difference between the height of the scope and the center of the barrel (the bore) is 2.15 inches. I'd taken the time to set up the bipod and still hadn't gotten enough clearance. A quick visual check would have made that clear, but I didn't think the time it would have taken to do that was worth it. At that point, I recognized the whole "haste makes waste" nature of my error. I'd gotten out of my usual rhythm and hadn't taken the time to do all the checks that I usually did.

I could have sulked about this and beaten myself up, but we had bad guys getting closer and assault teams to protect.

"Give me your pack," I said to Wayne. He handed me his tactical pack and I butted it up against the ledge. It gave me the clearance I needed. I rested the barrel on the pack and set up the weapon again.

Obviously, I was in a dynamic situation with things changing by the second. I needed to assess where our guys were. I could see that they'd detained a few suspects and were herding them outside the main objective. The bad guys were still in the irrigation ditch, spread out along a snaking line of that dried-up waterway for about twenty yards, from my eleven to my one. While I was assessing the situation, I heard the quick *pop-pop-pop* of an AK and a couple of rounds smacking off the sides of the building Wayne and I were on.

The assault team hunkered down for a second, and then one of them radioed up to me to check on our status.

"We're good."

"We're done here. Outbound ASAP," the GFC chimed in. By this time the assault teams and the detainees were all in single file line waiting for Wayne and me to clear their path of those three targets.

I scanned the area outside the compound. Two of the armed guys were still in that ditch, along with a third one whose weapon status I hadn't been able to confirm.

Of the three, he was least visible. Either the section of the ditch he was in was slightly steeper than the rest of it or he was much smaller than the other two guys.

"Got to go. Got to go. Got to go," I heard again over the comms.

I shut that out of my mind. I knew that we had a limited amount of time. The choppers were flying offset maneuvers, just waiting for us to come in. They were vulnerable to ground fire and surface-to-air. The assault team believed they had their guy. But I knew that unless I really took the time to do things right and take out those three bad guys, all the good we'd done so far might be wasted.

I got in my zone and fired the first round at the fighter nearest to my position. Too low by inches. The dirt flew just in front of him and he ducked. I stayed calm and moved down the line to the guy on the far right, the one who had fired on us. The round must have struck him in the throat. His weapon flew up, and I watched him clutch his neck for a second before he dropped out of sight. For some reason, the first guy stood up. Whether he was yelling at the third guy to grab the gun and peel back or something else I can't say. All I know is that he offered me a perfect target. I sighted in, dialed in, and delivered the shot.

He bent forward at the waist and clutched at his pelvis. I wasn't sure if he was wearing a breastplate, but if he had been, then I'd delivered an ideal shot. The hips and the midsection are particularly vulnerable if you can squeeze one in below the chest armor. It's a particularly effective shot, because so many digestive organs are nearby, along with the arteries and veins that feed them. A lot of blood flows out of those wounds in a short amount of time. Based on what I saw before the guy slipped beneath the edge of the ditch, he would bleed out damn quick.

The unarmed bad guy covered his head with his arms and made no move to pick up either of the AKs his buddies had dropped.

"Good to go. Good to go," I told the teams. "One additional bad guy. Unarmed and under watch. Good to go."

"Roger that." A moment later the call for the helicopters and extraction went out.

"Do your thing," I heard the GFC say.

All I had to do was watch that last fighter, and he didn't move an inch the entire time our team filed out of the compound. Wayne and I climbed down and joined the rest of our guys on the helicopter. As we flew off, that guy was still there in the ditch. I knew he wasn't dead; I could see his chest rising and falling. As we lifted off and then the dust cleared on his position, he stood up and watched us go.

One of my favorite parts of an operation was when we'd land at the airfield back home at our base. Some of the higher-ups would be there to greet us and congrat-

ulate us on a job well done. It wasn't like a formal cere-
mony or anything, but more like a team going from the
field to the tunnel that led to the locker room. It was
like the owner and the general manager and a few of the
other "suits" were there to let us know how much they
appreciated what we'd done. They'd put us in an environment and trained us up so that we could succeed. We
had. Whatever little miscues had taken place receded in
the immediate aftermath of the mission.

Still, I knew that, eventually, I'd get crap for those
two shots into the edge of the roof.

I also knew that it was probably time for me to fess
up to the rest of the guys. I'd let a few of them know
that I wasn't going to re-up. This was, unless something
truly crazy went on in the next few hours, the last operation I would go on as a member of the 3rd Ranger
Battalion or any other military team. I was done.

I'd chosen to not go wide with my disclosure. Timing is everything, as the saying goes. I didn't want my
departure from the military to be a distraction in any
way. I also didn't want to deal with the attention that
might have come my way. I guess, at least in hindsight,
I also wanted a bit of wiggle room—what if I changed
my mind? But now I was absolutely sure. I'd taken the
time I needed to reach a definite conclusion.

As we walked along the tarmac back to our quarters,
guys were in high spirits, celebrating the success of
the operation and the end of another deployment. I

don't know who exactly ratted me out, but when Austin mentioned that it was Wilson's last operation ever, my name and my circumstances got tossed into that same mix.

"Irv, you're calling it quits, too, huh?" Alvarez said, sidling up to me and bumping me with his shoulder. "Thought maybe you were going off to work with the dog teams," he added.

"Yup. This is it for me. Time's right."

"Gotta listen to your gut, Irv," Jones said. "Don't want to be out there with a case of the doubts."

"True that," Gordon said. He was one of the assaulters, a breacher with a huge appetite for eating explosions of all kinds. He had a collection of fireworks back home that would shame a small town's Fourth of July display. "We'll light some up in your honor, that's for sure."

His last comment reminded me of something. Just as we'd left the compound I'd heard the sound of special-purpose rifle rounds going off. A bunch of them, what sounded like a magazine's worth.

As we were walking I glanced over my shoulder and saw Kay, a monster of a dude with a linebacker's body and the aggressive mentality to match. "Who was firing suppressed before we left?"

A big old smirk spread across his face before he broke into a laugh. "Man, you will not believe what happened. We're making our way to the exfil point and I saw a bad guy about a hundred yards ahead of us. He was in the fighting position, hunkered down, and one hand was in the air and another was balancing on the ground. Looking for all the world like he's about to throw a grenade at us. Freaking guy had a helmet on, too."

"So you lit him up?"

"I did. Turned out I was shooting at a fire hydrant or some damn kind of irrigation thing. Tore that thing up!"

Everyone within earshot started laughing and hooting.

"That's why you're not a sniper," I said to him at last, once I regained control.

"No, that's why I'm a hell of a sniper. One hundred percent contact. Didn't miss a shot. Can you say that?"

"No." I shook my head slowly. "I can't. Right shot, but the wrong guy."

Kay laughed. "Good times, though, Irv. Right?"

I nodded, thinking that time would tell. It was too soon and not the right time in lots of other ways to put together an after action report on my career. Just then all I wanted to do was savor the feeling of having done our jobs and come home safe, and laughing with my brothers. There's a time and a place for everything in this life, but there's never going to come a time when I won't miss that sense of belonging.

Still, even in the afterglow of that operation, I knew that I was making the right choice by leaving. There was neither a time nor a place for you to be out there with any kind of uncertainty in your mind. Doubt and hesitation could lead you to mess up your timing. I'd messed up a bit on this operation because I was in a rush and didn't follow all the steps I should have. But in this case, I'd taken the time to truly consider what was best. It was time, the right time, for me to go.

NINE

MISSING THE ACTION

SOMETIMES IT'S THE OPERATIONS that you *don't* go out on that are the hardest to deal with. As a sniper, as anyone who's been with a team for a long time, you want to be there to help support one another. It's a lot easier on your nerves to be in the middle of the action than it is to be on the sidelines.

I also realized how hard it must have been for my family to know that I was out there while they were back at home waiting and wondering. Every time the phone rang I'm sure that their hearts skipped a beat and questions came popping up like the bad guys always seemed to whenever we were in Helmand. Long-range sniping is all about being patient and calmly waiting. The longer

I worked doing direct-action sniping, the more I realized that maybe that was what I was better suited for.

In early 2009, I was sitting with a bunch of guys shooting the shit. "You hear about my man LeBron? What he did the other night?" Lester jumped in. He was an assaulter who we liked to say was the only guy we knew who was a better shot out on the court than out on the range.

"Can't you see we're talking here?" Douglas said in mock anger. In fact, all Lester had done was cut short one of the recurring debates the car guys were having—synthetic oil versus dinosaur oil.

"Dude lit up the Garden. Triple double for the youngster out of Youngstown," Lester went on. "Incredible. Fifty-two points. Ten rebounds. Eleven assists!"

"Akron," Willis said.

"Stop trying to change the damn—"

"LeBron's from Akron, not Youngstown, you—" Thomas's insult was cut off by the sound of our pagers going off.

We scrambled from our seats. We'd heard a rumor that one of the regular Army groups in Helmand with us had been in a hellacious firefight. I think we were all hoping that we'd get the call to go into that same area and clear those bad guys out of there. None of us, at that point, had any idea just exactly what we'd be getting ourselves into. And, as it turned out, only a select few of us were going to be heading there; the rest of us were told to keep our mouths shut if we knew anything at all about the situation that had developed. Our superiors were on constant alert about how news got spread.

We knew that the war wasn't popular with the folks back home, but more than that we were all concerned about our loved ones and what they might find out about our status. Procedures were in place for how notifications of casualties and deaths were going to be reported to the families and to the media. Officially, we didn't want anybody to get a call from a reporter or anyone who wasn't tasked with the responsibilities of notifying next of kin in case one of us was injured or killed. Unofficially, we all agreed about keeping the media's noses out of our business, but like most guys, I'd had an unofficial agreement with Mike about how things should go down in case I got dusted or shot up. Neither of us wanted the doorbell-ringers to go to our loved ones to deliver the news. Even though our unit was good about sending somebody who, hopefully, knew us and could share stories with our family about us in case we were KIA, we knew that wasn't always the case.

It wasn't an easy thing for any of us to contemplate, but we'd already had one experience with losing Benjamin Kopp, so we were all keenly aware of the need to have contingency plans in place. Even the most hardened follower of rules and regulations was willing to bend them under worst-case scenarios.

I hustled into the briefing room, already geared up to

go, and felt my heart sink a bit when I saw the roster and realized that I wasn't on it. One of the other sniper teams, headed by a great guy named Perkins, was going out on point with a small team. The longer I sat there and the more I learned, the more I wished that I were going out there with them.

The regular Army unit that had gotten in a scrape with the Taliban on the outskirts of Kandahar had reported that one of their guys was now missing in action. Nobody had seen him get shot or anything. They did find his gloves lying on the ground, but there was no sign of him anywhere.

When I heard that, the hairs on the back of my neck stood up. Like everybody at home, I'd seen and heard stories about what the Taliban and al-Qaeda did to their prisoners. If this line guy had been taken, things didn't look good for him. We had to get out there and get him back ASAP. Normally, this was the kind of thing that SEAL Team 6 or the Delta Force guys would have taken on. But as things had been evolving in Afghanistan, our role as Rangers had been as well. The regular Army unit had put in a request for assistance and we were spinning up to help them out. Time was of the essence and all of that.

I didn't think much at the time or even now, to be honest, about who went through what channels to get approval for us to go after the guy. So what if that wasn't what we spent most of our time doing and had only trained to do briefly? One of our guys was in *their* hands. That's all we needed to know.

It sounds kind of selfish to say that I was pissed that the higher-ups went with the second sniper team guys. I understood that I'd been without a spotter for a while. Mike had broken his leg during a fall into what we now referred to as a "Mike Hole"—a kind of vertical subterranean tunnel that plunged him a hundred or so feet beneath the surface and required him to be rescued by the Combat Search and Rescue team. Brent had been rotated home a bit earlier.

Perkins was a guy I'd gone through all of my sniper training with and he was someone I liked and trusted. He and his spotter, Gillian, were more than qualified to do the work. I didn't question their capabilities, but I was still angry that I wasn't going out there. I understood intellectually that it was probably the right call. Given the urgency of the situation, it made sense to bring out an intact sniper team. Still, given the urgency of the situation, I wanted more than anything to be there. I didn't want to have to sit back behind the wire and feel helpless. As I sat there all kitted up and listened to one of the longest and most involved briefings I'd ever heard, my mind wandered briefly to ways that I could convince the powers that be to let me go out there with the team. When one of your guys is in trouble, it's natural to want to be out there to help.

I sat there taking notes just like I would have if I

were going out. We had our guy's name, his call sign, his social security number, and a bunch of other data about him that could prove helpful or not. The guys in the TOC were scrambling as well, trying to get us a photo of the guy gone MIA—Wilson. Soon, we had photos of his badge and his Army ID, and that was followed up with aerial images of the area in which he and his guys had been ambushed.

The images of that sector really got me thinking I wanted to be out there. Within a few blocks of his last known position were dozens of buildings, between forty and fifty. How that small team was going to go in there and clear each of them in a timely manner was hard to imagine. I'd seen the assaulters hustle their asses off and they always impressed me, but sending in so few men with so much at stake was troubling. How were Perkins and Gillian going to be able to move and provide overwatch for a team moving that quickly among that many buildings?

I knew that we wanted to go in light to avoid too much notice from and too many encounters with the locals. I also knew that if anything spun up elsewhere and another unit needed to go out, I was the lone sniper left on the bench. I kind of felt like that last guy on the team who couldn't be put in the game, who was held back in case one of the other guys got injured. We didn't want to operate shorthanded. I also knew that if things went sideways out there, I'd get called in for backup support. But as much as I wanted to be there, that was the worst-case scenario that no one, including me, was hoping for in any way.

I decided to do what I could to help, even if I wasn't going out there. I stayed in the briefing room for a few minutes after the meeting broke up, reviewing as much of what I'd learned as I could. I'd worked pretty closely with the guys in the TOC, so they had no problem with me coming in there and asking to see various live video feeds, recorded footage, photos, and anything else I needed to get a good sense of the lay of the land. I knew that the eyes in the sky would be operational, but having a sniper's perspective on things was different. I could communicate with my specialists in a way that no one else could.

I glanced at the clock and realized that Perkins and Gillian were probably just about to leave the ready room. I dashed down there.

Perkins was one of the rock-steadiest guys I'd met in the platoon. He was deeply religious. I don't know if it was his faith, his general temperament, or both, but I never saw him lose his cool and I seldom saw him in anything but the sunniest of moods. When he saw me, he smiled and gave me a quick nod of his head in recognition of what I was going through. He'd been on the other side of this situation, when I was getting all the calls to go out on the key operations.

"You're going to do this," I told him. "Know you're ready."

"We've got it," he said, indicating with a glance his spotter, Gillian. Perkins was shrugging on a pack and then bouncing up and down to get it to settle before he worked its straps.

"We'll have him back before chow time," Gillian said. I liked Gillian's confidence. He wasn't too much of a talker normally but now his voice came booming out. I realized that he must have had in his ear protection and didn't realize how loud he was speaking.

"Keep your heads down. Lots of possible hides for you and for them." I went on to explain that I'd seen a particular intersection where three roads merged like an arrowhead into a main thoroughfare. They needed to be particularly cautious.

"Thanks, Dad—I mean, Irv," Perkins said. I had to agree with him that I was feeling a bit like a father about to let his son go out and drive the car on a date for the first time.

Gillian came over and put his hand on my shoulder, "We're good. Appreciate it and all, but we're good."

"I know. I know. I'm just worried."

Since we'd lost Ben Kopp during an operation, I'd become more of a worrier than ever. You always understood that one of us could die, that you could be the one to be killed. But with Kopp's death, thoughts of our mortality had risen closer to the surface, had become far more real than some theoretical "it could be me." It made my insides tighten up every time I strapped on my body armor—which I was wearing at that moment, both in a kind of empathetic camaraderie that I can't really explain even now, and in the hope that I would get the last-minute call to go out there.

I went back to the TOC and looked at the maps again.

"This is going to suck," I said to myself, hoping that wouldn't be the case at all. As in most of the country's more urban areas, and a lot of the exurban areas, the buildings seemed to be placed haphazardly and not along a grid. There were a lot of offsets where one building stood slightly in front of another. All kinds of possibilities continued to run through my mind. I fought the urge to check in with a few other guys I knew. We suspected that somehow the bad guys could listen in on some of our cellular communications. We'd been ordered to go silent; I was sticking with that.

I had a couple of options, but sitting and watching the drone footage live was the best of them. I settled behind one of the monitors. I'd be able to get the big picture and to track our movements and the enemy's with that view. I watched the Chinooks—from the moment they took off from our base until they landed. The guys didn't exit the bird with the usual fast-hit urgency we employed when on most operations. Instead, they kind of went into tracker mode, immediately fanning out and walking slowly, hoping to pick up clues as to what had gone down and how and where Wilson might have become separated from the rest of the guys. They'd been dropped off about three quarters of a mile from the objective—a building that, based on the limited intel we had about movements and past activities in the area, seemed a likely location for them to have taken our guy. We were roughly four hours after he'd gone MIA. Intel showed no sign of anyone fleeing the area.

I watched as the team spread even farther apart. I imagined that they were hoping to encircle the building, blocking off any egress points from it. I also had an audio feed; hearing the snipers and the others communicate made me feel more like I was there—except I wasn't. My stomach was in knots and I was staring so hard at the screen that I had to force myself to blink. I couldn't identify individual guys from that eye-in-the-sky view, but I could definitely track everyone's movement. They were still in tracker mode, surveying the terrain, stooping and stopping to sniff things out as if they were canines.

They talked about finding brass—spent shells, mostly likely from an M4 or AR rifle like Wilson might have been carrying. They also debated a bit about how fresh the footprints they found were. What was most strange was finding just a few of those shells, when they'd been engaged in a major firefight. The whole area should have been littered with them. They also didn't find any spent AK47 shells. Weird. Was one American guy over in this area firing just a few shots? That didn't add up at all.

The guys in the TOC asked me what I thought. All I could do was guess. Maybe somebody had come into the area to clean it up, knowing that if we realized they had one of our guys, we'd sure as shit come down hard and fast on them to rescue him. Whoever did the cleanup might have missed those few shells. Or maybe they left them there as a kind of decoy? I was getting a bit frustrated because I wasn't on the ground checking these things out myself. As a sniper, you're kind of a detective—observing closely and making guesses about enemy positions and possible tactics. This was like watching a show on TV, but it was real life and a whole lot more was at stake than ratings and critics' reviews.

As they neared the objective, the guys pivoted and moved back in toward it, making certain that no one emerged from the more open area at their rear to ambush them. A small handful of guys, including my sniper teammates Perkins and Gillian, made their way to a narrow alley. I heard Perkins over the comms alerting the rest of the group to his position and to his intention to move down the alley and toward a building at a 45-degree angle to the main objective. My heart was pounding pretty quickly already, but when I saw the whole screen in front of me go white, I jumped out of my seat.

What the fuck had just happened?

All of sudden, a 70-inch screen erupts in a white flash? What could have done that? An RPG? Was it a camera malfunction? Not likely, since the picture was restored instants after that bright flash. Over the comms, the dreaded TIC acronym gets used over and over: troops in contact.

"It's really on now," I thought.

At least most of the guys seemed to be in good fighting positions. I also thought that I should get out of the TOC and get ready to be flown in there as backup.

Next thing I know, the letters "WIA" flash across the screen in front of me. Things are happening way too fast. We got a guy wounded in action? Who? What happened? Did that flash occur because of an explosion?

My question about "who" was answered in an instant. Across the bottom of the screen, the code name for "Perkins" was displayed. I switched channels on the audio to get the complete feed from our ground force commander, the guys upstairs with me, and all the guys on the team who were reporting back in.

Pressure-plate IED. The demolitions expert on the team had been able to identify the type of device by the wiring and a few other small bits of it that were left in the ground. A pressure-plate IED is set to a number of pounds of pressure, say 1,000. A device inside it tracks and totals the number of pounds of force that come in contact with it. So, to put it simply, once it is implanted, a kind of countdown begins. Once that total is reached, the 1,000 pounds in this example, it detonates. It was Perkins' shitty, shitty luck that he was the one who triggered it. It didn't make any sense, but I immediately felt like if I had been there, maybe it wouldn't have happened, maybe Perkins would have stepped a couple of inches to one side or the other, instead of where he had. Who knows, but that survivor's guilt thing kicked in immediately.

Next, I turned my attention back to the most important thing: How was Perkins doing? According to the reports coming in, he was conscious and breathing. We all knew from what the medics told us that there is a "golden hour" after a guy gets wounded that can make all the difference in his surviving or not. That's the amount of time between the initial wounding and his getting treatment in the hospital. Our medics were trained to get a guy as stable as possible so that he could be transported to the location of the best medical care. I knew that the Chinooks were coming in to get Perkins. I also heard some of the guys saying that Perkins would be fine.

That wasn't a whole lot of comfort, since we'd been told the same thing about Kopp, who died after taking a single round. Perkins had stepped on an IED and been blown up. He landed about forty feet from the IED; that had to mess some things up inside of him, along with whatever other damage was inflicted—I figured that he had to have lost a leg. I hated not being there with Perkins and the rest of the guys. I wanted to know what the situation was. I wanted to be there to offer whatever help I could. I wanted to be there to talk with him, let him know that he was going to be okay and that all of us were thinking good thoughts.

I decided that if I couldn't be there on the operation I could be there when Perkins arrived inside the wire. I hustled out of the TOC and went to our housing unit. I gathered up a few of the guys I'd once worked with on an assault team before I became a sniper—Coyle, Adams, Lefebvre, and Mason. I let them know what had gone down.

"Sounds like he's going to be okay," Adams said.

He was trying to do the right thing and stay positive, but I was so bent out of shape, I turned on him. "How the fuck do you know that? Are you there? Are you a doc?"

The guys all tried to rally, but I tuned them out. I didn't want to hear a word from anybody. All I kept thinking about was Kopp. He'd been two weeks away from going home when he got shot. Perkins was due to be out in ten days. Why was it that as guys got closer to *going* home, something happened to *send* them home? Was there some kind of curse?

"We gotta go, Irv," Coyle said, his tone making it sound more like an order than a request. Good—I needed somebody to take charge and snap me out of it. We climbed onto the back of a flatbed pickup and headed to the airfield. I sat there thinking that if any Military Police tried to pull us over and ticket us for speeding,

I'd chew the guy's head off. No one did, thank God. We got to the airfield and saw that the Chinook was already on the ground and was just sitting there empty. Still, we drove toward it, and then saw the line of guys hustling along the tarmac. Halfway there, I spotted the stretcher with Perkins lying on it, wrapped in a foil space blanket to help keep his body heat from escaping.

We detoured to the hospital and got there as a few of the guys from the team were making their way to the entrance. I recognized Gillian by the way he walked, how he seemed to be perpetually walking into a stiff breeze, his head behind the axis of his spine. Even before our vehicle came to a stop, I jumped out and made a beeline for him.

As I got closer, I saw that his face was covered in soot. His eyes were wide and he had the kind of dazed expression on his face you'd expect of a guy who was within a few feet of getting blown up.

"What happened? What happened?" I asked, close to screaming the words.

Gillian wiped his nose on his sleeve and looked at the dark smear before responding, "Irv. Dude." He shrugged, "Fuck me. I should have . . ."

He shook his head and then coughed and spat. "I don't know, man. I do not know. One second we're closing in on the objective, the next thing I know I'm seeing a bright white light and I'm knocked on my ass. I got to my feet and started looking for Perk. He was ahead of me a few yards when it hit—when he hit it or whatever."

We all resumed walking, wanting to be as close to Perkins as we could.

"Took a few seconds, but I found him in a ditch. He wanted me to check his junk, make sure, you know. Wants to have kids."

I knew that Perkins was a newlywed. His wife's name was Amy. Met her at his church back home in Missouri, someplace in the Ozarks, I thought.

"So I checked it out for him. And he says—" Gillian stopped walking and took a deep breath like he'd just sprinted four hundred yards. "He says, 'All right, you can let go now.' We both started laughing, and I was hoping that was a good sign, you know?"

Gillian had radioed in for help and in the meantime checked him out. The thing that had most scared him was that Perkins' eyes seemed to be crusted over, like maybe they'd been blown out by the concussive wave and then filled in with dirt and stones and other debris.

"I didn't want to touch them. Didn't want to look at it. Fuckin' mess. He kept asking about where his night vision was. Told me that he couldn't see a damn thing. Man, that would suck if . . ." He let his words trail off.

"So, I told him no, he just had some stuff in his eyes. Told him he would be fine. He got quiet for a bit. I don't think he lost consciousness, but maybe he did."

By this time we'd reached the hospital. The guys

who were gathered there stepped aside to let Gillian by, knowing that we were sniper team and should be with our boy.

"He's in there," one of the guys said, nodding toward a doorway.

I shouldered it open and was immediately really pissed. Perk was on an exam table and just beyond him I could see two Taliban guys lying on other beds, IV drips hanging down from their holders. I didn't know when they'd been brought in, but having them in close proximity to Perkins so soon after what had happened to him just seemed wrong.

I remembered a conversation I'd had with Perk a few weeks prior to this. I was complaining about this exact thing—how we treated their wounded and how they would most likely let us suffer and then die a horribly painful death.

"You can't go around living your life like that," he said. "Hating people isn't going to get us anywhere. Sure isn't going to get us out of here."

That made me think. But seeing him lying there all busted up next to those two bad guys was making me think again.

I walked up to Perkins and put my hand on his chest. "Hey, Perk."

"Irv," he said, turning his head toward me. He smiled. "You doing good?"

In that instant I did a quick assessment of him. What

Gillian had said about his eyes was true—that area of his face was messed up. It kind of looked like cauliflower and gravel and ketchup all mixed together in small lumps. I had to look away. I saw his right hand. It was bandaged and the gauze was soaked with blood. It was so soaked that it had almost gone completely transparent and I could see the gaping wound that seemingly butterflied his hand in two.

"Irv, man. I don't know what happened out there."

"I was watching the whole thing on the drone feed."

"I figured. You should have been there, man." He tried to keep it together, but a smile started to leak across his lips. It was good to see he was trying to rip me for how I'd acted before they left, my whole dad thing. I couldn't let him know that those words hurt—and that I was thinking the exact same thing.

"Are you good?" he asked, filling the short silence that had come over us.

"Yeah, I'm good," I replied. He asked about the others, starting with Gillian. I knew he wanted to hear from the rest of the guys, so I called them into the room. It seemed like his main concern was for the rest of the guys; I knew that's where his heart was. Still, I had to wonder if he was really okay or just under the influence.

"You on the meds, Perk? That why you're feeling so good?"

"No, they haven't given me a thing. I'm just grateful."

One of the doctors came in and asked us to step aside for a few minutes. They understood after taking care of us for so long that this wasn't like your usual hospital setting. We were going to be there in the room for a lot of the time and they were okay with that. We just needed to keep out of the way.

A few of us stepped outside into a small waiting area. We stood, barely talking, mostly just lost in thought, thinking about Perkins and his eyes. He was going to survive, we were all pretty sure, but what would it be like to not be able to see?

At that point, Mack, our first sergeant, came in. He was a hard-core dude, as I've stated before. A guy I'd flat-out just feared for a long time before developing a deep respect and admiration for him and for the fifteen-plus-years he'd put into his career and the countless hours of heavy-duty combat he'd endured. I'd seen the University of Georgia football team play a few times on television and they always showed the team's mascot, a big old ugly bulldog name Ugga. Every time I saw Mack, the image of that dog passed through my vision. Now imagine that kind of face streaked with tears coming at you. I felt my throat clamp shut and tears welling in my own eyes. Mack reminded me of my dad. I'd never seen my dad cry until the day I left for my first deployment. When guys like that can't hold it in, you sense you've been granted permission to let go yourself.

I followed Mack into the room, where he stood at the foot of the bed. He took a deep breath and stared up at the ceiling.

"I'm sorry," he managed to choke out.

For the first time, Perkins seemed more like a patient than the guy doing the cheering up. The emotion in the room was thick. I watched as Perkins' face muscles twitched and spasmed for a moment before he stilled them.

"You'll want to call your wife," Mack said. He held out a cell phone.

I knew that Perkins couldn't see the phone to take it, let alone dial it. I walked up to my sniper buddy and said, "I'll hold it for you, Perk." It took all the strength I had to get those words out. He was still bleeding badly from his hand. His legs were under a sheet and I couldn't see what kind of damage had been done to them, but I figured it was likely bad.

I could hear the phone ringing and ringing, and then I heard Amy's voice-mail greeting. I hung up immediately. If she had caller ID she'd see the number and know immediately that it was him. I didn't know if she was the worrying type or not.

"Not there, Perk. We'll try again in a few," Mack told him. I did the math in my head. We were nine and a half hours ahead of central time back in the US. It was five-thirty in the morning here, meaning it was eight o'clock Saturday evening there. Where was she?

The doctor had administered a painkiller. With the help of that and the blood and IV fluid being dripped into him, Perkins was looking better.

"What do you remember?" someone asked him.

"A flash of white light," he said, and kind of scrunched up his face thinking and trying to recall more. "I think an angel must have saved me."

Knowing Perk as well as I did, I knew he was having some fun with us. I decided to keep it light. "Dude, you did not see an angel or a light. That flash was a bomb, dude."

"No come-to-Jesus moment for you," someone else added, sounding like the Soup Nazi character from *Seinfeld*.

Everyone, including Perkins, cracked up.

Finally, after three or four more attempts, Perk's memory kicked in. "She's at Bible study. She'll be done at eight, walking out to the car at eight-oh-five. Maybe a little after if she chitchats with Pastor Steve for a bit. She'll have her phone on then."

I could relate to his knowing to the minute where she was on any given day. I was the same way with Jess. It wasn't a control-freak thing, but when you deal with the kinds of things we do, you learn to keep tabs on your loved ones. ICE—in case of emergency—is something you take seriously. If you care about somebody, you keep track of him or her, both downrange and at home.

Finally the call went through. Mack was holding the

phone now, and even before he had a chance to speak, Amy said, sounding so happy to hear from Perk, "Hey, honey! Wasn't expecting you."

Mack identified himself and gave her the few details that he was allowed to. Her husband had been hurt. He would be coming home. Someone would be in touch later with more details about his flights and arrivals. The rest was, at this stage, still classified. She could speak with him.

I took the phone from Mack and pressed it up to Perkins' ear.

It was a weird kind of invasion of privacy that also felt completely natural, given how tight we all were with one another.

I held the phone. Perk's tears and the mud and the blood from his eyes dripped onto my hand. I turned my head away, as did the rest of the guys, to give them some privacy, such as it was. I went into sniper mode and tried to lock out all thoughts and senses of what was going on in the room. I didn't succeed completely.

Perk pulled it together and at one point after he'd told her again and again that he was okay, he said, "Just stepped on some stupid little bomb. Couldn't wait to see you, so instead of going home when they told me I would, I decided to speed things up."

I had no idea how he found the strength to make those jokes and keep her as upbeat as he could. He even managed to slip in some of the details about his condition without alarming her too much. "Just got some stuff in my eyes. They're going to wait a bit, then flush them. Hey, did you get a chance to get those tires rotated on my truck? Tell those guys not to scratch those rims, please."

I looked down at Perk's hand and hoped that it would be okay. I looked at his eyes and hoped that what he was telling Amy was true. I remembered that before I went downrange, anytime I'd wake up before Jess, I'd look at her and touch her lightly from head to foot. I wanted to see and feel every inch of her. I wondered how different it would be to go home with a prosthetic and not a hand, to have my sight lost or impaired. How would I deal with that? How would people treat me? How bad would Jess and my mom and dad feel? Would they experience guilt and similar feelings because they hadn't been there? Would they believe, like I did, that if they had been present things would have turned out different? How many more times could I step on my own kind of pressure plate before it went off out there or inside me?

When Perk was done talking with Amy, I handed the phone back to Mack. I stayed with Perk for just a few minutes more. I needed to get out of there. This was all too much for me: the emotions, and the questions creeping up on me from all sides.

"I'll probably be gone when they fly you out of here,"

I told him. "I'll be checking on you, though, you know that. I'll see you when I'm back home."

As it turned out, Gillian also went home. As with most things about our time in Afghanistan, Perkins' injuries were a good news/bad news kind of thing. Eventually, though quicker than I'd expected, he recovered completely from his wounds. His hand was sliced up bad and fractured but, thankfully, with a few metal plates and screws it was put back together and functioned fine. His eyes were fine, too. For a few weeks the docs weren't sure if his vision would be affected, but it wasn't.

The most frustrating thing that resulted was we learned that the guy we had thought was captured, Wilson, wasn't missing at all. He was young, and everybody was so freaked out by the ambush that had occurred, they messed up the roll call. He had never gone missing. That kind of stuff shouldn't happen, but it did. I didn't want to think about the "what ifs" in regard to Perkins. I guess those angels he was talking about weren't MIA in his case, but they sure as hell were with that regular Army unit. Maybe somebody upstairs was trying to test the faith of all of us.

It confirmed something I already knew: I wanted to be out there, not back inside the wire. I wanted to count on my guys and me, not trust in things that I couldn't see or feel or otherwise observe firsthand. That's what it meant to be a sniper, and it was a good thing that Perkins would be able to return to the action with his senses and his faith intact. I guess that, like I usually did, I preferred to travel a bit lighter, but whatever other guys needed to carry along with them to make it through was just fine with me.

TEN

AFTER ACTION REPORT

I WAS IN that intermediate zone between asleep and awake. Strapped in like a kid in one of those Johnny Jump Up gizmos, I rocked and swayed along with the Chinook on the air currents. It was hard to hear over the sound of the rotors and through my ear protection; just a faint buzz and murmurs were all that penetrated my fogged mind. I looked around the cabin. Most of the rest of the unit was asleep or at least had their eyes shut. Mack was on his laptop, his face lit by the screen's glow. He was staring at the maps and images being fed to him, his eyes darting around the screen. What passed for a smile appeared on his face. He caught me looking at him. "Target's clear!" he said over the sound of the rotors and the engine. "Target's clear!" He pointed at the screen, letting me know that he was watching the live video feed. Whoever had been near the objective had moved off.

I gave him the thumbs-up. This was good news. Wade and I would be able to make it onto the roof I'd selected.

We were all bathed in red light. It was a surreal scene, I guess, but it had been part of my reality for so long it seemed natural. I closed my eyes and focused on my breathing, hoping that something like rest would overtake me until the countdown came over the comms and before the tightness in my belly, something close to hunger pains, consumed me.

That red color was so much a part of my world that even just a few days ago, now nearly seven years on from that last firefight I was about to engage in on the very last night of my very final deployment, I stood at the counter of my local grocery store and suddenly I was back on that Chinook. One instant I was looking at pieces of fried chicken under a similar-colored warming light, the next I was flying over Afghanistan, hearing the white noise of the rotors and the motors. Weird that all it took was the sight of that color to transport me from one world to another. I continued to wait my turn and as I stood there, another memory came back to me. I was back home in Maryland watching TV in the family room with my dad. Me sitting on the floor with my back against the couch, him in his easy chair. He and I watched things on the History Channel, a few PBS specials, retrospective looks at Vietnam and World War II mostly. I was watching them primarily for the battlefield footage. I wanted to see the action. When they cut away from those scenes to interview some of the participants, it seemed to me that those guys were way, way old. And they always seemed to get too wrapped up in what they were remembering and they'd almost all get choked up and fight against crying or actually shed tears.

One night while watching those interviews with my dad, I looked over at him and asked, "What are they crying about? All that stuff happened to them so long ago."

My dad shook his head a bit, narrowed his gaze at me, and took in a deep breath through his nose. His lips pursed, and I could see him thinking deeply. I looked at him and then at the screen, waiting for action in either place. Finally he said, "You don't get it. You can't get it." The words came out flat and factual—no condemnation, no residue of resentment. He reached for a chip or some other snack he had sitting in a bowl on the arm of his lounge chair and chewed thoughtfully for a second. "Some things just stick with you," he said at last. He didn't say any more, and the screen filled with the image of a helicopter, triple canopy, and huts in a clearing. Showtime.

The people ahead of me in line seemed more like they were deciding whether or not to pull money out of their retirement fund to buy a business than choosing how many pieces of white meat or dark meat they wanted. I had to check my growing impatience and the urge to lean over the counter and box up my order myself. Burning daylight, folks. Is it really a dine and dash when you carry the food out?

Then I realized that I didn't really want to rush home. I knew that Jess would see me and sense immediately that something was up. Then I might have to explain. Then I might have to be like one of those vets on one of those TV shows. It wasn't so much that I didn't want to cry, it was more like I wondered if maybe I was no longer capable of it. And if I didn't break down in front of her, would that say more about me than if I did?

The phone call had come from Mike; we still checked in with one another every week or so. He let me know that Alex Fernandez had put a gun in his mouth, pulled the trigger, and ended his life. Alex was my first squad leader when I was the cherriest of new guys with the Rangers. He was stone cold and worked hard to get me squared away. He'd chew my ass out for any failure to be the best soldier I could be, but he let me know that I should wear the honor of his attention like a medal: If he didn't think you'd end up being worthwhile, he didn't bother with you at all. He set a good example for me and a lot of the credit for whatever success I'd become was due to him.

I'd talked to him only a couple of weeks before this. I asked him how he was doing and he sounded so proud of himself. Getting A's in all his college classes. "Doing good, Irv. Doing real good."

Now he was dead, and he was the shooter.

Whose definition of "doing good" was that?

Then, as Mike and I finished up the rest of the call, we did what we always did as Special Ops guys. We talked about what we'd observed, speculated about what we might have missed, went over what we did and what we could have done better. We'd lost one of our guys to suicide, after learning of another who'd taken his own life just a few weeks earlier. What did you see happening with these guys? What did that tell you to do? What plan of action, what tactic did you think to employ? Then, individually and collectively, Mike and I beat ourselves up. We should have been there for him. We could have prevented that. We should have seen that coming. We're Rangers. We're snipers. We're trained to notice, to act preemptively. Anticipate. Analyze. Plan. Enact.

Only we didn't.

Only we couldn't.

Now Alex was dead and what we had to do was figure out a plan for honoring him.

After action reports had been so much a part of our lives for so long. The later our deployments were in the Global War on Terrorism the more we were asked to justify our actions, second-guess ourselves, analyze, and reflect. Relive those moments, record them for the official record, and always, always hold ourselves accountable. We had to prove that it was a good kill.

To this day, Mike and I go over operations, think about the things we could have done better, wonder about how things might have gone different if we'd done X, Y, or Z instead of

A, B, or C. I purposely use letters here, because the conception that many people have of snipers and sniping is that it is a simple numbers game. Get the numbers right and the bad guy goes down. Truth is, the Minute of Angle is a constant, but human beings are not.

I had an instructor in one of my sniping courses who always used to say, "The bullet doesn't lie." He'd say that all the time, but especially when one of us trainees said that we had done the math right. We didn't see how we could have possibly missed that target. That miss didn't make sense. That couldn't have happened. I did the numbers.

But it did happen.

We did miss.

Bullets don't lie.

What had we missed about Fernandez? Bullets don't lie, but shooters do?

I remember when I was first downrange in Iraq and we'd be helicoptered to an insertion point. The dust would be flying and you'd step out into that cloud and wonder and trust that the ground would be there to meet you. I heard stories of times when, for some guys, it wasn't and they step out and fall dozens of feet. Eventually, the procedure got changed. I thought of that on the night of that last firefight after my brief exchange with Mack. The Chinook's crew chief wouldn't let anybody out until we were safely settled in the moon dust. Still, I'd step off and into that cloud, put a foot forward tentatively, wondering if somehow we'd been dropped in at the edge of a cliff, a ditch, a cesspool. It was an irrational fear—the pilots wouldn't do that to us. Still, it was one I felt that night and on a lot of other nights before and after.

People ask me all the time what it takes to be a sniper, a member of a Special Ops team. I never answer this way, but I know that one of the things that I find funny in looking back on my time with the Rangers is how much of the time I was afraid and worried. I've stated this before but it's worth repeating: I hate heights, am scared shitless by them, but still, I never failed to get on a chopper, a plane, or even to jump from one. I felt the fear but did the thing anyway. What that says, I'm not sure. I can't say that I'm an adrenaline junkie or that I have a death wish, because neither of those two things is true. I just knew that I was with a bunch of other guys who were going to do this thing, and so was I, so I followed the guy ahead of me and did it. And I felt good while doing it. So, what I say in answer to that question about what it takes is that you have to like to challenge yourself. That's a nice way to phrase it. Maybe this: You can't be afraid to be afraid.

The night of that firefight in Afghanistan, I wasn't looking for a challenge necessarily. This was going to be one of those quick in-and-out missions like so many others were supposed to be and wound up not being. One unique feature of the operation was that we'd be heading out toward the mountains. The compound backed up against some rocky cliffs and walls. I wondered why they would do that. I'd felt tremors and quakes a few times in Afghanistan and Iraq. I imagined that place getting smashed up beneath an avalanche. I would have thought those bad guys would have considered that possibility, but didn't consider in my initial assessment that maybe they knew better than me.

On that operation, I was interested in putting Wade to the test a bit. He had decided that he wanted to be a sniper. He'd stepped into the role as my spotter and done great work with me. Whether it was making sure that all my mags were fully loaded and doing it without making any kind of deal about it, or just generally busting his ass and doing everything at a rate of speed and efficiency that had me shaking my head in admiration, the guy was everything the Rangers needed him to be.

Still, I kind of looked at this last operation as a way for me to be sure that I passed along to him, like other guys had for me, whatever knowledge and experience I'd gained in my time as a Sniper Team Leader. Unofficially, among those things was this: It is a far, far better thing to be inserted onto level ground free of irrigation ditches than it is onto one that has them. I was grateful that night of my last-ever operation that I wasn't going to have to do the balance-testing mud run along those sons-of-bitches ditches. I wasn't feeling nostalgic at all that night, and especially about those thigh-burning, lung-searing exertions. Run for the fun of it? Not me. That night, though, we covered the two miles in an easy lope across level terrain. Thank the Lord for small favors.

The only thing that worried me was that as we came out of the dust cloud, I wasn't able to see the guys ahead of me; I'd lost my place in the formation. I called out for Wade, and he responded immediately. He was right behind me, just where he was supposed to be.

"We're good. We're good," he said. "We'll form up."

Even prior to this dusty whorl of an insertion, my worst thoughts were that I'd get off a bird, run in and through that cloud of dust, hear the sounds of a firefight, see guys with weapons, let loose my own, and before I know it half my team's on the ground because of me. Never happened, thanks to the fear that it *might* being front and center in my mind, keeping me from doing something so fundamentally stupid.

Wayne and I did form up with the rest of the guys, and then we split off from them, just as planned, making no contact with the enemy. "Just a quick in-and-out, exactly as we drew it up," I kept telling myself. "That's what I want for this last one." Then back inside the wire and in a few hours on our way home. Deal with what "home" really means when we get there. Outback Steakhouse and its Bloomin' Onion. New York Strip. Sour cream. Potato. Good things. Good things. Think good things, not bad things.

I looked around me. The compound we were going after was nestled in a wide valley, the buildings backed up against the steep and rocky rise of mountains higher than any I'd ever seen before—Everest-high, it seemed.

I'd never seen mountains like this before, and as I hustled along in the darkness, I thought this was a place of great beauty. Did people come here for vacations?

Stop being a tourist and start being a sniper, I told myself. Those aren't mountains, those are places where prime fighting positions are a dime a dozen. Figure out the one that you'd select—maybe the bad guy would make the same choice as you. Anticipate, you dumbass. You're vulnerable down here in the valley. No cover. No concealment. They could be up there and they could pick us all off one by one. Mack said, though, that it was all clear. Have to believe he's right. Have to be prepared in case the intel wasn't.

The compound started to take shape the nearer we got to it, mirroring the satellite imagery we'd reviewed. Now, in the rock and dirt of it, that photo image becomes real and I located myself in it much better. I nudged Wade and gestured to the building four hundred yards away and at our two o'clock. He nodded and unstrapped the ladder in preparation for our climb.

A few minutes later, we're at our building. This wasn't going to go to plan, though. A slit trench carrying raw sewage runs parallel to the building a mere six inches from the wall. Our only option is to put the ladder up tight to the wall, giving us about an 87-degree to vertical-climb up that ladder. No way that ladder touches that nasty stuff in the trench. No way. I remembered what happened to a guy we all called Q when he swallowed human waste and water, and that's not happening to Wade or me.

We're about to mount the roof of the building and were about to take our overwatch positions when I hear a very loud boom—not coming from our flash bombs—a different sound but one I recognize.

"RPG. RPG," I say to Wade. We both hit the dirt, careful not to get into that trench, and heard the RPG fly overhead and then impact a few hundred feet beyond our position. Twice in my career I've had an RPG fired on my position. This would be the last time, I thought, as I picked myself up off the ground. Hugging those ladder rungs, pressing myself against them as tightly as I could, using my body armor as a slick surface to ease the friction, I inched my way up and then onto the roof.

"Use your armor as a sled," I told Wade. In sniper training we used ladders all the time in drills. Out here is where you learn what you really need to learn, and you figure out solutions to problems you would have never predicted you'd have. I low-crawled around the lip of the building's roof, mindful of possible shots coming up from below. Wade did his zigzag for the same reason, looking a little like a speed skater at the start. We both got to our positions safely. I noticed that Wade had pulled the ladder up behind him. Smart. No one was going to grab it; no one was going to use it to come up there; no one could see it and report our position. I've still got a thing or two to learn.

I thought a while longer. How are we going to get down from here?

Jump?

Again with the fears? Heights. Disease. Is that the sound of locusts I hear?

I radioed to Mack and to our GFC Duns to let them know we're in position. We go into overwatch of the assaulters; if those guys are the tip of the spear, we're the shield. I watch their orchestrated movements, them doing things I've seen them do dozens and dozens of times before, but still marvel at. What's the word?

Synchronization.

That's the sense that all the individual pieces of the whole are functioning together. I allow a thought in: I'm going to miss being part of this, miss the sense that, at least for a little while, everything in my world is aligned, all the parts are meshing.

Funny thing was, I talked to Mack shortly after I heard about Fernandez. We all knew that guys killing themselves was a kind of plague, taking way too many of us way too young. It's a disease, something that we have to steel ourselves against and fight off, develop some defenses against, some immunity for. Feel the symptoms. Get a diagnosis. Seek treatment. Simple as that, but so much more complicated than that.

What do we do? How do we help each other? How do we get guys to open up and talk when we don't really want to talk ourselves? Mack said that he thought that some of us had lost our sense of purpose. What do you do when the thing you'd spent most of your young adulthood training to do is no longer useful or possible or even legal? We were trained to kill. Were the guys killing themselves in some sick way doing what they'd been trained to do? Hold it all in. Destroy the enemy.

Bless him, Mack said that he believed, and I believe he believed this, that keeping the body in shape would help guys out a lot. As the body goes, so goes the mind, he said. Healthy body. Healthy mind. Build yourself up. Look at the Spartans, he told me, those legendary warriors of early civilization. They carried shields that weighed fifty pounds. You guys complained about two and a half pounds of armor. You've got to be strong. You've got to be able to protect yourself.

We're not talking about deflecting arrows, hammer blows, and spears, I tried to tell him. Besides, we bitched about the armor but we used it. We knew it helped us. But what do you do when you're no longer inside or outside the wire and still wearing armor that the Army didn't issue and most folks don't even see that you have on?

Mack didn't say this, but I thought about it this way. Control. That was what a lot of us loved about what we did. Doing PT was a part of that. Discipline and control. Get your body to do what you wanted it to do. Kind of like wanting to challenge yourself. You couldn't go into battle thinking that your body might fail you. Make it do what your mind and your will told it to do.

Most of the guys I knew in Special Ops were what some people might call control freaks. I hate that term. Why is it that somebody who likes to take charge and have command *of his circumstances and hold himself accountable for events and the consequences of his choices and actions is considered a "freak"? Because we were at the far end of the scale in that regard, did that make us unnatural, make us mutants, someone to be avoided or feared, someone who threatened everyone else? I know that sometimes I felt that separation in civilian life. Us versus them. We'd seen it and done it and nobody else could possibly understand but us. And if I can't tell one of us because I don't want to seem weak, don't want to put doubts in their mind about whether they can rely on me to have their back, then who do I turn to?*

We had made contact, and the enemy was wielding a fair amount of firepower. The assaulters were in a good defensive position. No one was in anything close to direct line of fire. The bad guys were doing their usual show of force, popping out around a corner, firing randomly, just a lot of noise and fury amounting to very little but a nuisance. I wasn't doing too much engaging, acting mostly as an observer calling out movement of targets from building to building. I was trying to figure out if there was a pattern, if they were coordinating a move to some rally point within the compound. Nothing I could figure out, just a random bunch of moves, but at least they were away from our main objective.

The assault teams were given the order to proceed. The enemy is running and gunning, but at least the noise is receding. Another sound spreads across the night. The reports coming from the signature control rounds our assaulters were firing were sharper, more precise in their timing and shorter in duration, almost like Morse code. I could tell that those rounds were coming from a building to the east of the main objective. If they were firing rounds there, we weren't doing much to support that team from our present location.

"I'm on the move," I told Wade.

"Roger that," he said, and got to his feet, indicating with a quick hand gesture that he was going to follow me.

The narrow gaps, no more than two feet, between the rooftops made leapfrogging from one to another very easy. Even if someone was below us and wanted to fire a shot up that gap, it would take incredibly bad luck on our part, or good luck on theirs, to hit us. Obviously, if we heard automatic weapons fire coming from below and through that gap, we would have halted and held our position. We only made a few jumps before we took a knee and reassessed.

Below us, on an adjacent building just off to our left a few degrees, I saw what looked like mosquito netting slung across the rooftop. I thought I could make out the shape of a couple of human figures on it, like they were guys sleeping on a large hammock. I'd seen odder things than that before and was used to finding locals asleep outside to avoid the heat, oblivious to the gunfire going on nearby.

"Get your infrared," I said to Wade. "Light that area up."

Wade produced the flashlight and clicked it on and then shined it on the position I'd indicated. Through our night vision, it seemed as if one those huge spotlights that car lots or other businesses use to light up the sky was illuminating that rooftop. The figure below—it turned out to be just one guy on that netting—couldn't see it at all. But he must have detected something, because he opened one of his eyes. It looked like when a dog's eye catches some light and then glows brightly. It did that for just an instant and then he shut his eye and his whole face seemed to dim. We had to make a call. Wade and I stood there for a few seconds. The guy didn't move at all. I felt like I was looking down on some kid who suspected the bogeyman was in his room and had pulled the covers up over his head and slammed his eyes shut hoping that whatever he'd just seen would just go away.

I looked at Wade and shook my head and then pointed with the index and little finger of my left hand to my eyes. Wade nodded. We'd keep an eye on the roof man but do nothing more unless needed. Suddenly, from out of my peripheral vision another figure emerged, this one running from south to north on a diagonal between Wade and me and the objective. I tracked him briefly until I heard Wade yell, "Gun! Gun! Gun!"

The rooftop man had rolled over in order to stand, and I could see the white glow through my night vision of the barrel of his AK47. I pivoted with my weapon and in a fraction of a second my scope was filled with the image of his clothing and a belt. He was no more than fifty yards from me, and he dropped an instant after I squeezed the trigger. Had it just been me up there and my attention got diverted to the runner, the rooftop man would have blown me away. From fifty yards his pray and spray would have been effective on me as well as on the assault team, which was moving, without knowing that guy was there, into position just to the east of where he'd been lying and waiting in that netting.

I didn't have too long to think about how bad things could have turned out. A few seconds later, a third guy, one that neither Wade nor I had spotted before, came running on our position. He veered left, south to southwest along a row of buildings. I couldn't tell if he was armed, but based on past experience I knew this: If he was running toward the buildings, he wanted to stay engaged in whatever was going on. He was hoping to get inside one of those series of doors he was passing. If he just wanted to be safe, he'd have chosen to go in the first one he came to. He didn't. He was determined to get into a specific building. That meant there was something inside that he wanted bad enough to risk getting shot. If he was just an innocent guy caught in the crossfire, he would have headed the other direction, out and away from us and out toward the nearest edge of the compound and into the fields beyond it. Most of the time, that's what the noninvolved locals would do. That's what

I would do if I was in that same position. Get out while the getting's good.

All of that flashed through my mind in an instant. Next thought was this—I can't let him get where he wants to go. If he's unarmed now, let's keep him that way. If I put a few rounds in front of him, just to kind of put up a stop sign out there, I would accomplish that goal. I knew that with the ROEs I couldn't take him out, but I could keep him from getting to where he wanted to go and getting what he wanted to get. I also knew I needed to put those rounds as close to him as possible to let him know that they were there, that they weren't just some random rounds coming from somewhere indeterminate. He needed to know I saw him, was targeting him, and could take him out if I chose to.

It was a risky shot, to be sure. He was on the move, and that always complicated things. I couldn't count on him keeping up a steady rate of speed, and he was moving at a slight angle to my location rather than perpendicular to me, so his distance wasn't a constant either. If I was off a fraction in my calculation or in my technique, I could have hit him. My military career was just about over; I was anticipating being on a plane bound for Germany within hours. If I didn't do my job right—if I hit him—I'd have to face the review board and admit that I'd shot an unarmed local who posed no immediate threat to me. I'd face a dishonorable discharge and possibly jail time. If I let him go about his business, who knew what he was up to, what kind of damage he might do, what kind of havoc he might wreak.

I aimed just in front of the runner's face and fired. All the time I was aiming, Wade was behind me. I was in my zone and not communicating with him, but he was telling me, "Decrease degrees. Decrease degrees." He thought I was trying to hit the guy and could see that I was off a few degrees in my aim. A human head is on average nine inches across. I wanted to be just about two to three inches ahead of that while figuring that the guy was at seventy yards away and moving away from me, increasing his distance slightly. He was more than half a football field away, roughly two ninety-four-foot basketball courts in distance from my position. All three rounds impacted off the wall just ahead of him. He sank to the ground, tucked into the fetal position, and stayed there. Perfect shots. I'd done what I'd done hundreds of times on the shooting range going after wooden targets. I'd kept my weapon set and moved my body incrementally, keeping them on the same plane.

My attention was taken up next by the sight of the two lead assaulters bearing down on the stopped bad guy's position. I figured they'd round him up, but they ran right past him.

"Damn it!" Wade was clearly pissed. If that guy had a pistol on him or a grenade or some other kind of explosive, this could be a bad situation.

Wade got on the comms immediately and relayed

the cowering bad guy's position to the team members. The two lead guys who overran him came to an immediate stop and retraced their steps. They were joined by a few others, all of them with their weapons up and on him, shouting at him in Pashto.

With so much going on, I didn't have time to alert the assaulters to the existence of the second guy. They knew about the one on the roof I'd taken out, but not the runner. From our position, it seemed like he was right there in the open, pinned against that wall. But when you're running along like those two other guys were, with night vision making it tough to see with complete clarity, I could understand how they'd missed him.

Wade wasn't as understanding of his teammates' misstep. "How the hell did they miss him? They just moved past a guy who could have killed them. He was a potential threat."

"Controlled chaos, right?" I said. "That's why we're up here. We still had a line on him. If he had done anything but stay down after those guys went past, one of us would have taken him out. That's why we're here. We did our job. Had their backs."

"Still. They should have."

"But they didn't. Things happen. You miss stuff. I've missed it a bunch of times. You cover for each other."

"I know. But damn it." Wade was still pissed, but I think that more than anything he was afraid of how he would have felt if something had turned out bad. He didn't want to go there, so he got angry as a way to deal with all the bad stuff bubbling up inside of him.

Later, when we got back on the chopper for the ride back, I'd have another chat with him. I'd come to think of us as guardian angels, but this was not the time for it. And I didn't think it would ever be time for me to talk to him about not being afraid to be afraid.

I heard more percussion grenades and flash bangs, the sound of our machine-gun fire. Over the comms I heard that the clearing operation was going well. At a few spots I could see our guys standing security over a few zip-tied locals. Reports came over the comms about the number of prisoners being taken. It was a good haul, and it seemed as if this one was winding down.

We got off the roof and helped out the guys IDing the dead guy and gathering intel by assisting one of the machine gunners with providing security. As soon as that was wrapped up, we remounted the roof nearest to us. Persistent gunfire was still coming from the extreme northern end of the compound. Not steady as in a fire-fight but enough to let me know that we were needed in that direction.

"Let's go hopping," I told Wade.

That seemed to lift his spirits and take his mind off of what might have happened. After a couple of hops due north, I caught a glimpse of a lone gunman out in the field beyond the compound that led to a steep rise, kind of like a ramp that took you to the edge of a sheer rock face. He was about 250 yards out, based on the *crack-thump* rough estimate I came up with while setting up; with the mountains and the buildings inside the compound distorting the sound waves, it was nothing but a ballpark figure at that point. I figured he was inside the AK47's 380-yard effective firing range, but it would still be a very tough shot for him to make contact with our guys. You never knew when an unlucky round would find its way on us, though. I didn't want to get any closer to him in case he spotted us, so we dropped down at that point and set up the classroom. I seldom did this, but I wanted Wade to see exactly what I was doing. I narrated a bit of what I was doing so he'd get a better understanding.

First, I surveyed the scene. Our guys weren't pinned down by this gunman. They had taken up good defensive positions behind these sled-type wagons without wheels the locals used to haul hay and other supplies around. We risked exposing our position by firing on the guy, but based on everything I'd heard to that point, he was the only target left. I didn't think that anybody would be coming out of the so-called woodwork. We were good to go on him.

Second, I determined the range more accurately. Using the vertical method, since I could see him from head to crotch only, approximately one meter or 39 inches, I placed the crosshairs on his waistline and measured to the top of his head. The difference between the two was

3.5 mils. Using the formula, I took the 39 inches and multiplied it by the constant 25.4 to get the number of meters and divided that by the 3.5 mils. He was 309 yards out, a good 50-plus yards beyond my rough guess using sound. In training we'd been told about sound distortion and mountains, but this really drove the point home. To make sure of the range, I did a quick shoulder-to-shoulder measurement on the guy, used the horizontal formula, and confirmed the range. Trouble was, the guy had moved slightly to his right, taking up a position partially behind a rock. All I had left to me for aiming was his head.

I got into the supported prone position, using the roof's raised edge to rest the bipod on. I settled in, closed my eyes, opened them again, breathed out slowly, and then squeezed the trigger. The bullet didn't lie. I knew as soon as I saw it leave the barrel that it was going to miss. Even using both those formulas, at night and with my night vision on, calculating the height of the target was tough. From that distance, an inch or so of inaccuracy in determining his actual height or width was going to throw off the numbers. I wasn't fazed by the sound of that .308 round smacking off the rock in front of the guy. In sniping, I told Wade, it's all about the second shot. "One shot, one kill" doesn't usually work out in the field.

We were in what I learned in Sniper School is called the "Honeymoon Period." That's the few seconds before the target can process everything that's just gone on in his world. From the time I squeezed the trigger to the time I squeezed it again was a matter of three to four seconds. In that span of time, the guy could move out, but this guy didn't. He flinched but raised up again. While he was doing that, Wade was behind me telling me that I needed to hold up .3 mils. I knew the adjustment I had to make, but it was good to hear Wade calling it out.

The round found its target—and that was the last shot I fired in Afghanistan on that deployment, though at the time I didn't think about that much. We radioed in to let everybody know that the target was neutralized. They went about their business, Wade and I lay on the rooftop, feet to feet, me pointing to twelve, him to six, making sure that we had 360 degrees of coverage for the guys.

While we waited for the helicopters to come in for the exfil, I watched as the prisoners were led up to our position. They were all bound with zip ties. A couple of them were crying and a few had wet themselves, dark stains running down the front of their clothing. I didn't feel bad for them really, but I wondered for a minute what it must have been like for them. They were scared, obviously, and their lives were about to change, had been changing over the course of the last few minutes. Now was the big unknown. What are these people going to do with me? What's it going to be like to be separated from most of the people I've been around for so long?

Maybe I'm just slow, but at the time I didn't realize that those guys and I had a lot in common. My life was about to change radically in the next few hours as I made my way home, leaving behind a group of guys who'd been as much like family as my own, guys who shared something with me that my family and friends back home would never understand. As our guys placed the bags over the heads of our prisoners and shut them up in a dark cocoon, I wondered briefly what their future might look like. Would they be bitter and resentful and angrier? Would they see the light, maybe emerge with a new vision of what was possible for them?

I didn't have a whole lot of time to think about it. The choppers had come in and I had my guys to watch out for. Later, back inside the wire, the word came down that we'd have one last inspection before we climbed into the minibus to the airfield. We knew we'd better straighten our rooms—another group of our brothers was coming in and we wouldn't want them to have to clean up our messes.

I don't think my wife would say that when I arrived home from any deployment we went through any kind of "Honeymoon Period"—no honeymoon, period, might be more like it. After this last one, we came into Fort Benning from Germany and got off the plane. I'd been enjoying my time on the flights, alternately sleeping or messing around a bit with the guys. As soon as we were back on the ground, the fun ended. I was back to being the team leader, a sergeant, somebody who had to set an example.

As we filed onto the bus that would take us to our head-quarters, I'd already steeled myself for the greeting. I'd seen other guys cry when they saw the wife, the kids, the family. Not me. Wasn't going to do it. When the bus stopped and the brakes belch-hissed and the door rattled open, I was Iron Man. I had no superpower other than going numb. I'd walk past the long line of eager greeters and catch a glimpse of Jess out of the corner of my eye, waving a sign and jumping up and down. I'd keep on going, hurrying to get to the ready room so I could unpack and stow my weapons. Had to take care of my babies. Had to keep it together. Wasn't going to cry. No. Not me. I can't lose it here in front of all these people. Not in front of my guys. I'm still Irv. Nick can't come out yet.

Jess found me and wrapped her arms around me and hugged me. The smell of her was foreign, sweet and spicy in contrast to the gun oil and the plastic smell of our Pelican cases. At first, my joints felt unyielding, mechanical, as I brought my arms up to hug her. She wanted to hold on so tight and for so long, and I felt like I just wanted this to end. Now. That's enough. Shut it down before the tearing in my throat and the itching of my eyes and nose overpowers me.

"Let's do this later, Jess. I've got things to do."

She nodded and dabbed at her eyes, turned around and

let me do what it was I needed to do. I felt the fear, and was afraid to be afraid. I didn't want to walk out of that room, offered to help every guy with the smallest of tasks. I wasn't ready to leave. Wasn't ready to be Nick. Didn't know if I remembered how.

A couple of flights, from Afghanistan to Germany and then Germany to the US, aren't enough time to make the transition. I don't think traveling those distances on foot and on the sea would be enough.

Weeks went by. I'd get up early some mornings and go outside. The smell of diesel being carried on the cool morning air brought me back. I'd be stepping off a helicopter and making contact with the tarmac. I'd start thinking as I stood on the sidewalk overlooking the parking lot of our apartment building, "If I'm getting off this bird, then what was it that I'd just done?"

Don't want to go there, but I did. Every day. Sometimes all day. It's a habit. It's ingrained in you. It's a part of the routine.

After action reports are a part of every operation. I did this. I took up this position. I fired. I killed. And because I killed, I was also subjected to additional reporting—more paperwork, more interviews. Go through the details of it over and over again. Never enough details for them. You can't escape the feeling that you're being asked to justify your actions. It's only natural, at least for me, to start to question myself, to second-guess. I'd look at my interrogators' faces and sometimes see the judgment in their eyes and wonder if they'd ever been in my shoes. I knew that for sure I'd never want to be in theirs. If they couldn't understand me and what I'd had to do, then who could?

Felt like a kid in the principal's office. Can I go now? Just give me the detention and let me out of here. I'd trained myself to compartmentalize, to put all those thoughts and feelings in their own high-impact ballistic plastic boxes and stow them safely away. Why do I have to open them now, again? What if I can't get all that stuff back in there? What happens if it all spills out and my emotions become like squirters? Am I going to be the one who has to track all those targets and take them down before they do some harm?

Command and control. That's what we do.

One night Jess asked me to talk with her about what it was like. She could see that I'd been struggling and was distant. She wanted me to be happy and to really show it. My responses to her were flattened. I love my wife and I wanted to honor her request to talk about it; I just wasn't sure how far to go. I guess I went too far, because at one point, telling her about how important it was to me that I be as good of a sniper as I could be so that my shots took the bad guys out and they didn't suffer, she shook her head and clamped her hands over her ears and was shaking her head so fiercely I thought she was going to hurt herself.

I understood. I didn't blame her. Who wants to hear that there were times when your husband was out there somewhere saying, "Damn it. Please die. Please die," while hoping he didn't have to put another round into an enemy fighter whose motives and morals he didn't understand and didn't care to.

Fernandez took his own life on his birthday. Imagine that. Imagine what must have been going on in his mind.

Thing is, I can. One day, Jess was off at work. I was feeling stressed. I'd neglected to pay our electric bill. Money was a little tight, I was out of it and not employing my usual situational awareness, and I'd let things slide. At breakfast Jess showed me the disconnection notice.

"I'll take care of it," I assured her. I wanted to be the one to take care of the bills. I'd handle it.

After she left, I panicked. I had no idea how to resolve the situation. Do I call somebody? Is there somewhere I can go and hand-deliver a check? What the hell do I do if suddenly the lights go out, the TV grows dark? How could I have let things slip like this?

Hours—I'm not even sure how many hours—later, Jess came home and found me. I'd made my way through an entire bottle of whiskey. I don't remember much, but she told me the next morning when I was more coherent that I was sitting in my easy chair, my pistol in my lap, and I was out-of-control crying, telling her, "I don't want to do this. I don't want to do this." To be honest, I'm not sure if I meant I don't want to shoot myself or I don't want to keep on living. I do know that I felt useless and isolated. Even when Jess told me what I'd been doing, I just sat there and shrugged. I could have told her that I'd thought of doing it a few times before, *but what would be the point of that? What was the point of anything?*

Then she said, "I can't sit here and do nothing. I need help in getting you help. I'm going to talk to your mom and dad." Somehow that penetrated my defenses. I sank down on the floor and begged like a little kid, "Please don't tell my mom. Please don't tell my mom."

She told my mom, and I love her for that. She and Jess and my dad arranged for me to see a therapist through the Department of Veterans Affairs. It wasn't easy, but I managed to open up a bit. Then a bit more. It was kind of like sniping in a way. One shot wasn't going to find the center of the target. It took her acting as my spotter, guiding me and helping me account for all the factors that went into getting to the heart of things. Over time I started to feel better, felt more like a human than an alien, learned that not being afraid to be afraid worked in Irv's world and mine.

Eventually, I told her about Ben Kopp, about the guilt I felt about his death, how I'd been carrying that with me for so long.

She said that she was sorry that I had to go through that. I appreciated the words, but compared to what Kopp had endured my burden was nothing.

She told me that I needed to give myself permission to let it go.

My mind understood, but my heart and my soul would never agree that was the right thing to do.

As I drove home from that therapy session with her, I

remembered these words from General Schwarzkopf: "The truth of the matter is that you always know the right thing to do. The hard part is doing it."

A few months ago, I was able to do something I'd not been able to do for nearly ten years. I was visiting my mom and dad in Maryland. We were having a good time. My mom is a woman of a deep and abiding faith in God, and she credits my turnaround to His intervention. I was due to fly back home to Texas on Monday. Sunday morning, I got up and went to church with my parents. It was a warm spring day. The dogwoods and the azaleas were blooming. My mom was planning my favorite meal, lasagna, biscuits, and gravy, for dinner. I was looking forward to it, but decided that I had something I needed to do. I'd be back in time for dinner, I told them.

Arlington National Cemetery is a special place. That's a huge understatement, obviously. My words can't do justice to it, so I won't even try. It took me a bit of time, but I managed to find the site I was looking for. On my very first deployment to Afghanistan as a Sniper Team Leader, I was on an operation in which our squad was pinned down by a Chechen sniper. I'd been selected to go along on this op to take him out; he'd been wreaking havoc on our guys. During that engagement with him, he wounded our platoon leader and killed Benjamin Kopp. Kopp was a good guy and an even better friend, and earlier that day he had saved Mike and me and a few other guys with his heroic actions. That Chechen sniper had all of us pinned down in a fairly steep trench. Kopp was two positions down from me when he got hit.

Every day since then, I've thought about Kopp. I've replayed that incident over and over and over in my mind. I've done that alone and I've done it with Mike. We "what-if" the hell out of those hours, performing a kind of slow torture on ourselves because if only one of us had taken up a position a few inches to the left or the right, Kopp wouldn't have wound up in the path of that bullet. Actions have consequences, and the collective result of all that we did that day produced a devastating result. We lost a guy.

Worse, I wondered what if I'd been able to take out the Chechen earlier. Then it wasn't a matter of inches. He wouldn't have had the opportunity to take aim at any of us. I would have succeeded and he would have failed.

I was given the title "The Reaper," and I gradually accepted the name. I also came to terms with the reason why I was given that name. I don't regret killing any of the people that I did. I did what was necessary and what I was trained to do. I'm working on getting over all the collateral damage that came my way because of those kills. I accept that as a natural consequence of my actions.

The reason I was at Arlington to visit Kopp wasn't that I was hoping to lay to rest the feelings of guilt and remorse and regret that I have over how I, in any way, contributed to him losing his life. As much as I went over and over the actions I took that day, I didn't ever really feel the loss, the gut-heaving, breath-seizing, bowel-ratcheting sadness of it. I was afraid *that if I did, every bit of who I was as a soldier, a Special Ops warrior, would come flooding out of every opening in my body and I'd no longer be me.*

I went to Arlington to apologize to Kopp for that. In many ways, I'd been doing him a disservice, not truly honoring who he was and what he did and what he stood for and what he died for, by not letting go and allowing my humanity to express the profound sense of loss I felt.

I stood among all those heroes and sensed that I didn't belong there, not yet. I was going to have to earn my place there, earn their respect and honor them by living as full a life as I possibly could. Kopp and thousands and thousands of others have made the ultimate sacrifice, and I hadn't been living the gratitude they gave me. I'd wanted to end my life, and that would have been rejecting the opportunity they'd worked so hard to present to me and to all of us. I also want to honor the guys like Fernandez and so many others who struggled in ways I can understand but whom I'll never judge. I hope that maybe by writing about some of what I went through, I can help my brothers in arms.

For a long time I was proud of what I did. Now it's time for me to work on being proud of the man I am and who I'm becoming.

I understand better now why those guys in the TV shows I watched with my dad reacted the way they did when they talked about their war experiences. There are some things you never get over. What I've learned, and what is maybe the most important lesson for a sniper, is that that's a good thing. Combat and killing change you. In sniping we calculate lots of distances, using constants and formulas. What you can't ever fully account for is a human being's power to make choices, to change directions, and to see things from another point of view.